Gettin' Old Still Ain't for Wimps

Karen O'Connor

Guideposts®
New York, New York

This Guideposts edition is published by special arrangement with Harvest House Publishers.

Cover by Cindy LaBreacht

Karen O'Connor: Published in association with the literary agency of Books & Such, 4788 Carissa Avenue, Santa Rosa, California 95405

GETTIN' OLD STILL AIN'T FOR WIMPS

The Library of Congress has cataloged Harvest House Publishers' edition as follows:

Library of Congress Cataloging-in-Publication Data

O'Connor, Karen, 1938-
    Gettin' old still ain't for wimps / Karen O'Connor.
        p. cm.
    ISBN-13: 978-0-7369-1771-1 (pbk.)
    ISBN-10: 0-7369-1771-3 (pbk.)
    Product # 6917713
    1. Older Christians—Religious life. 2. Aging—Religious aspects—Christianity.
    I. Title.
    BV4580.O357 2006
    248.8'5—dc22   2006001336

Printed in the United States of America

For my grandchildren...
who keep my funny bone working!

Acknowledgments

I want to thank the following men and women for sharing their touching, humorous, and tender experiences with me—many of which provided "seeds" for the stories in this book.

Marie Asner • Amy C. Baker • Millie Barger • Ralph Bender • Nargis Bunce • Janet Burr • Shirley Carson • Marge Carter • Glenna Clark • Joan Clayton • Dolores Collins • Eleanor Cowles • Dean Crowe • Mona Downey • Lorraine Espinosa • Pat Evans • Sylvia Everett • Pam Farrell • Lana Fletcher • Mary Lou Flinkman • Annette Freligh • Freda Fullerton • Vernette Fulop • Joyce A. Gendusa • Millie Gess • Judy Gilboe • Alice King Greenwood • Peggy Hamburg • Jeanette Hanscome • John and Edie Holm • Marsha Hubler • Angela Hunt • Shelley Hussey • Patti Iverson • Veda Boyd Jones • Susan Keck • Mary Kirk • James Lamb • Judith Larmon • Brad McBrayer • Mary McCormick • Jim McEldowney • Joan McMahon • Louisa Godissart McQuillen • Karen Milam • Sharon Moore • Sherrie Murphree • Marilyn Prasow • Naomi Rhodes • Sharon Riddle • Mary Beth Robb • Martha Rogers • Nancy Rose • Joanne Schulte • Joyce Seabolt • Margie Seger • Theresa Sheppard • Shirley Shibley • Ruth Sigmon • Shirl Thomas • June Varnum • Stephen Walsh • Helen Weeks • Marion Wells • Gary Winters • Brenda Woodard • Jeanne Zornes

Contents

A Note from the Author

Bette Davis once said, "Old age is no place for sissies." Indeed! It takes grit and wit to keep standing when your skin doesn't fit the way it used to, when you think someone stole your car but in truth you forgot where you parked it, when your grandchild looks at your figure and observes aloud, "Grandma, you look like a teenager—except for your head!" or "Grandpa, why does your neck jiggle when you talk?"

I hope you'll enjoy this all-new collection of original, lighthearted stories and inspirations to warm your heart and tickle your funny bone, just like those in the first book, *Gettin' Old Ain't for Wimps*. Included are scriptures and prayers to nurture your spirit and turn your eyes to the One who made us, who numbered our days, and who promises clearly that he will never leave us nor forsake us—right up to our last breath...and beyond.

—Karen O'Connor

Lookin' Purdy!

Hair Ye! Hair Ye!

Jane looked in the mirror at her straggly hair. "What am I going to do with you? I'm getting fat, and you're getting thin. It's not fair!"

She raked her fingers through the gray strands, remembering how her late husband, Terry, had loved her hair when they first met. It was golden then—and thick. Now at age 60, it needed all the help she could give it—perms, thickeners, a weekly shampoo and styling. But nothing gave it the look she wanted. When it came right down to it, she was losing her hair and there was no getting it back.

Jane dressed for the day, and then checked the mailbox. The carrier usually arrived around nine o'clock each morning. She pulled out a handful of envelopes and leafed through them. Bills, flyers, ads. *Nothing exciting here.*

Then a catalog caught her attention. The model on the front smiled from the page. *Her* hair was gorgeous, thick, flowing, wavy—just what Jane wanted. The headline beneath the picture beckoned: "WIG ISSUE—SEE INSIDE FOR BEAUTIFUL, NATURAL HAIRPIECES."

Just what Jane used to have and was now desperate for. She

13

tore through the pages, her hands shaking. Could this be the answer to her problem? A wig. *Why didn't I think of it before? Thank you, Lord. You always provide.*

Jane grabbed her credit card, dialed the 800 number, and talked to a representative about the perfect wig for her. After their consultation, Jane made her choice and placed the order. She hung up and looked at herself in the hall mirror. *I'm on the way to being a new woman. No more plain Jane!*

She kept her purchase a secret from her daughter, Kim, who lived with her, and from her best friend, Dotty, who lived across the street.

The wig arrived on Saturday while Kim was on duty at the hospital. Jane tore open the package and pulled the hairpiece over her head. *Gorgeous!* She couldn't help but touch the soft curls and run her hand through the gentle waves. She loved the sheen and the texture and the way it felt. In fact, she was sure she stood taller and looked much prettier than she had in years.

She decided to debut her new wig the following day. On Sunday morning she walked into the kitchen. Kim looked surprised and then delighted.

"Mom, you look *fab!* A wig, I presume."

"Ah," Jane mumbled, "I hoped it wouldn't be *that* obvious."

"Mom, get real. You've hated your hair for years."

Jane shrugged, grabbed her purse and keys, and headed for the car.

She drove to church in silence, but she noticed Kim looking her over and smiling.

What a morning. By the time they returned home Jane was flying. Angie had said she looked great. Barbara said she nearly didn't recognize her. And Dotty stood back and yelped, "Jane, it's a new you. I love it!"

By mid-week, Jane was so attached to her wig, she wore it from the moment she woke up till she went to sleep. It needed a small size adjustment, but she didn't want to part with it long enough to send it back.

The following Friday morning, Jane stopped at a coffee shop while doing errands. She ordered a cup of mocha and a muffin, and then sat down to read the paper and relax. It was a warm day, and the steaming beverage made her hot! She fanned her face with the menu and felt trickles of perspiration run down her face. She ran her hands through her hair to cool off.

Suddenly she realized something was wrong! She reached up. The wig was gone. She panicked.

"Looking for this?" a gentleman asked, stifling a laugh.

"Yes, and thanks," she mumbled.

Jane grabbed the mass of moist curls and ran out of the shop mortified. She prayed no one she knew had seen her.

How humiliating, Lord. How can I wear this thing? It can't be trusted!

At the car Jane took a deep breath, pulled on the wig, and checked herself in the car mirror. Then she got the giggles. Soon she was laughing so hard she was shaking. "God, is this funny or what? I'm remembering the scripture that tells me that you know the number of hairs on my head. Do the ones on my wig count too?"

Reflection

Indeed, the very hairs of your head
are all numbered (Luke 12:7).

Thank you, Lord, that I can cry with you...and laugh, as well. You are so good to me, caring for my every move, my every desire, my every fear, my every insecurity. I am so glad you are my Father, my protector, my provider. Because of you, I can find hope and humor in everything that occurs.

Tattoos Too

Millie awoke from breast cancer surgery groggy but grateful it was over and she was alive. The following day, Doctor Weston gave her the okay to leave the hospital. He scheduled her for the first of 28 radiation treatments to be given over the next several months.

On the day of her first appointment, Millie felt like a biker in a tattoo parlor. The lab technician painted purple dots on the area of her breast to receive radiation.

"Don't wash them off," Ms. Gonzalez stated. There was no mistaking her serious tone. This was an order! Millie complied. She had gone this far; she wasn't about to resist now.

Months later she walked into the lab smiling in relief. This was to be her last appointment. The lab technician once again dotted her breast with purple dye—without asking permission.

"Keep these," she said, "so we'll know where to apply treatment when you come back."

When I come back? Millie didn't care for the certainty in Ms. Gonzalez' voice. Not *if* you come back, but *when*.

Millie made up her mind at that moment. There would be no *if* or *when*. She had walked through the trauma holding on to the Lord, and she would keep going with his hand in hers and never look back.

Today, after 12 years of being free of cancer, Millie looks at her breast and chuckles. "The teens in town have nothing on me," she boasts. "I have my own tattoo—I just don't advertise it!"

Reflection

The name of the LORD
is a strong tower;
the righteous run to it
and are safe (Proverbs 18:10).

Lord, it's amazing how quickly a problem can disappear when I turn it over to you, when I look at the brighter side, when I rest in your arms, and when I find a bit of honest humor in what might appear to be a life-threatening experience.

Lookin' Good

Grandma Elsa, Phyllis' grandmother, always fibbed about her age. She got away with it because she looked younger than her years. Her husband died when Grandma was 53. To look at her then, she appeared about 40. But her fibbing created a real problem in the family. It made it difficult for Phyllis' mother and aunts to tell their true age because Grandma would have been taken for a child bride!

According to Phyllis, "The saga of 'Grandma's age' went on through the month she was eligible for Social Security. Grandma timed it so she was the last one in the Social Security office on the day she was to fill out her application. Instead of stating her age aloud, she wrote it on a piece of paper and handed it face down to the clerk. He flashed her a knowing smile as if to say, 'This will be *our* little secret.'"

But there came a time when Elsa's game backfired. At age 80 she met a gentleman of 63, who assumed by her looks that she was around 60. She did nothing to dissuade him of this thought!

The two dated for several months and soon everyone in her family was sure Clem would pop the question any time. Then one evening, while standing in line for a movie, Elsa's purse fell off her arm and the contents spilled on the ground.

Clem bent down to scoop up her lipstick, comb, breath mints, and wallet. There was her driver's license in the front plastic pocket of her billfold. Clem remarked on the photo, and then looked stricken. There was no mistaking her age from the birthdate printed in plain view.

That did it. Clem took Elsa home that evening, and she never heard from him again. "I guess a 17-year difference on Grandma's end was just too much for the 60-plus youngster," said Phyllis, chuckling at the picture in her mind.

Her grandmother died four years later, and even then Phyllis said her mother couldn't bear to end the fibbing. She shaved off ten years when she sent the obituary to the local newspaper. The editor, herself getting up in years, understood and went right along with it.

"To me Grandma Elsa will always be ageless," Phyllis stated. "She was just that kind of person—forever young in heart."

Reflection

Is not wisdom found among the aged?
Does not long life bring understanding? (Job 12:12).

Lord, I like to joke about my age, even to fib a bit for the fun of it. But the years we are on earth are nothing to you, for you are above and beyond the bounds of time. You love us with an everlasting love. You have promised us an eternity of days with you when we pass from this earth.

Soaking Beauty

Louann's mother, Mabel, a retired hairstylist, always took pride in washing her own hair using the same long hose in her beautician's sink that she used with her many clients. However, Mabel's 89 years and her arthritic fingers made it difficult for her to continue the practice. According to Louann, "Mom's too proud to admit she needs help so I suggested an alternative." Louann was sure it would work for her mother as it did for her.

"Mom," she suggested, "have you tried washing your hair in the shower?"

"Yes," Mabel snapped, "and it was awful. I couldn't breathe. Water and shampoo ran all over my face. I thought I was drowning!"

Louann put a hand to her mouth to hide the smile that broke across her face.

"Mother," she said softly, "did you *face* the showerhead?"

"Well, of course. I leaned right into it. Anything wrong with that?" Mabel was clearly insulted by these elementary questions.

"Mom, next time, put your back to the showerhead and lean

back. The water will slide down your hair, and you can shampoo and rinse without a drop touching your eyes!"

"Oh! Now why didn't I think of that?" Mabel chirped.

The two had a good laugh and a big hug. Gettin' older just got easier for Mom and daughter.

Reflection

Help the weak, be patient with everyone
(1 Thessalonians 5:14).

———————

Dear God, as we grow older it's hard to admit we could use an extra hand. We like our independence. We want to keep on keeping on by ourselves, thank you very much! But when we must rely on others, help us embrace what you have provided through a trusted friend or relative or maybe even a kind stranger.

Front and Center

Mary, the church organist, called early one Sunday morning as Ruth and her husband were preparing to leave for the first service. "Ruth, can you cover for me? I'm feeling ill."

Ruth was happy to help out, even though it meant rushing around at the last moment putting music together.

It was a hot and humid day so this added to the last-minute stress. The temperature had already reached 92 degrees at eight o'clock. "I knew I'd be sitting on a keyboard bench for over an hour," said Ruth. "The thought of wearing panty hose was unbearable.

"Then I remembered my sister had given me a can of Air Stocking to spray on my legs when I want to appear that I'm wearing hose or sporting a great tan. It also helps cover my veins."

Ruth rushed out to their sun deck and sprayed both legs up and down. She loved the idea of looking good and being cool at the same time.

On to church! She and her husband arrived minutes before the service began. Ruth jumped out of the car and raced ahead of John so she could get situated at the organ. Suddenly, she felt her husband's hand on her shoulder.

"John pulled me aside and chuckled. 'Ruth, I thought you used the spray on your legs?'"

"Of course I did. Look for yourself." Ruth felt indignant that he'd question her now, when she was in a hurry. "I glanced at the front of my legs, and they looked fine to me," said Ruth.

"Check the backs and just below your knees," John persisted, pointing and laughing. "I can see the line on each side where you stopped!"

By this time he was laughing so hard he had tears in his eyes. Ruth admitted she was mortified. "My skirt wasn't a mini by any means, but it wasn't long enough to cover my mistake either. By then there was no time to return home and undo the damage. It was one day when I hoped no one would pay any attention to me!"

Ruth remembered a passage in scripture that reminds us not to ask the Lord to guide our footsteps unless we are willing to move our feet.

"That morning," she said, "I moved my feet all right, nearly running to the front of the church."

Thankfully, no one said a thing to Ruth about her "interesting" leg wear. Her husband, well he's another matter.

"He continues to tease me about my one-sided hose!" Ruth says with a laugh.

Reflection

[He] gives grace to the humble (Proverbs 3:34).

Dear Lord, how embarrassing are those moments when I am suddenly exposed—whether physically or emotionally. I want to crawl in a hole or bury my head under the covers rather than face someone's judgment or ridicule or laughter. But then I think about the way you were humiliated and mortified on earth. You always remained humble and contrite. Thank you for your example.

All Moussed Up!

Donna and Roger's grandchildren live in Illinois so the grandparents don't see them nearly as often as they want to. "We make the ten-hour trip from Kansas twice a year if my husband is up to traveling," Donna said. "Last November we spent a whole week with our son's family. It was wonderful. I hated to leave."

Roger also had a great time. Donna was hopeful he'd want to make the drive again in a few months. He couldn't stop talking about the fun he'd had with his grandson Daniel, almost ten.

"Danny's very much like his grandpa. He's curious about everything and loves to ask questions, the serious kind that make you scratch your head before you answer," Donna shared.

One morning Danny hung around the bathroom door watching his grandfather work hard at combing a wave into his thinning gray hair. Roger gave up after a few tries. The flighty strands just wouldn't cooperate. He walked into the living room and settled on the sofa to read the newspaper. Danny followed.

Roger patted the seat next to him. Daniel plopped down beside his grandfather, looked up at him with curious eyes, and then popped a serious question. "Grandpa," he asked with a thoughtful expression on his face, "have you ever thought of using Mom's mousse? It makes *her* hair wave. Maybe it could do the same for yours."

Roger dropped the paper he was reading and about died laughing because that was the last thing he'd ever do! He was Mr. Clean and Simple through and through.

"Danny," he quipped. "I couldn't do that or I'd be *moussed* up for the rest of the day!"

Reflection

His hair is sprinkled with gray,
but he does not notice (Hosea 7:9).

Dear Lord, my grandchildren crack me up! They say the funniest things when I least expect it. I realize I need them around for more than one reason. They keep me sharp and focused and up-to-date on what's happening in the world—even the world of fashion and hairstyles.

Beautician or Magician?

Lana and Lou walked through their hair salon one last time. Lana began weeping. They had owned the place for 50 years and had served a clientele that spanned the county. In recent years they had added a service for seniors with special needs, including washing and styling and manicures in a separate room suited to people who needed a wheelchair or walker. That brought even more customers into their attractive shop on the west side of town. But now they were not only seniors themselves, but *elderly* seniors and running a business had become too much. It was time to sell the shop, retire, and relax.

They didn't worry about their own beauty needs because they could still do each other's hair. In fact Lana had depended on Lou for such help throughout their marriage.

Lana pulled a photo album from the shelf above her station and began paging through it, pointing to one hairstyle after another and chuckling when she saw the many changes that had occurred in the last five decades.

Lou joined her and had a few laughs himself. "Those were some get-ups," he said. "And we went right along with it. Amazing."

Curly perms, bangs and bobs, hippy hair-dos, and butch cuts.

The book included a wide range of styles that had come and gone.

Lou reached for the coffee cup on the table at his station. He read the wording and burst out laughing: I'M A BEAUTICIAN, NOT A MAGICIAN."

"Do you remember who gave it to you?" Lana asked.

Lou scratched his head and frowned. "Vaguely. Can't pull her name, right off."

"Marybelle Simpson," said Lana. "You got so upset with her one day that you let it out. 'What do you think I am, a magician?' you asked. Marybelle couldn't be happy no matter what you did." Lana paused for a moment and smiled. "For Christmas that year she gave you this cup. She was so excited about it. It was one of those items a person just happens on. You both had a good laugh."

"Never did like the beauty business," Lou mumbled.

"What did you say?" Lana's eyes revealed her surprise.

Lou raised his voice. "I never liked doing hair—never."

Lana was shocked. "What are you saying? *Now* you tell me—after all these years? What did you want to do? And why didn't you speak up?"

"I wanted to paint—you know, watercolors—but I figured I couldn't support a family on it."

"I'm upset thinking you were unhappy all these years, and you never owned up to it. What a waste." Lana's heart sagged.

"Oh it wasn't a waste, dear," said Lou with a twinkle in his eye. "I got to spend every day with *you*."

Reflection

Let beauty treatments be given to them (Esther 2:3).

Dear God, we don't always get what we want in life, but what does it matter as long as we have you. Spending time in your presence is all that counts.

On the Road

Joy Ride

Don's mother is 81. When he and his wife, Roxanne, visit her, they generally drive their Honda Gold Wing motorcycle from San Diego where they live, to Don's mother's house in Santa Cruz.

"During a recent visit," said Don, "I could tell Mom wanted to say something. But whenever I asked her if she was okay or if she had something on her mind, she brushed me off with 'I'm fine.' So I let it go. Then on Sunday after church she finally spoke up and asked me to take her for a ride on my motorcycle. What a surprise! She had told me to be careful so many times that I thought she hated the sight of it. She seemed terrified I'd kill myself. Now here she was practically begging me to take her on a joy ride.

"My wife grabbed Mom's kitchen step stool, and we helped her into the seat behind mine, put my wife's helmet on her, and buckled her in. Then off we went for a short ride around her neighborhood. Mom squealed like a teenager.

"'Now I see why you love this so much,' she said over and over. It was a kick to listen to her. I could only imagine the look on her face."

After Don and his mother returned, his mom asked if he'd take her on a ride along the ocean the next day.

"Once more we got out the step stool, loaded her up, and off we went. I don't know if I've ever seen my mother so carefree. It was fun for me to watch. Now I know where I get my young-at-heart attitude about life."

The following day Don and his wife and mother said goodbye. "I could tell Mom hated to see us leave," said Don. "If she were a few years younger, I think she'd have been ready to purchase a Gold Wing of her own. But then *I'd* be the one to shout, 'Be careful! You hear me?'"

A few weeks later Don invited his mother to visit him and his wife in San Diego. "Will you pick me up on the motorcycle?" she asked.

Don laughed out loud. "Mom," he said, "I'm not sure you're ready for *that*. An eight-hour drive on a saddle seat is not the same as a casual ride along the beach for a half hour."

"All right, I understand," she said. "But when I get there, will you take me for a ride around the block a few times?"

"Even more than a few, Mom—as many as you want."

Reflection
I will bless them and
the places surrounding my hill (Ezekiel 34:26).

Lord, what fun it is to kick back and enjoy the wind in my hair and the sun in my face, whether I'm riding around town on a motorcycle or napping in the hammock in my backyard. You have sent showers of blessings into my life! I want to enjoy every one of them with the people I love.

Keyed Up

Irene hurried out of the grocery store, holding her umbrella and car key in her right hand and her sack of groceries in her left arm. She dodged puddles and nearly lost her balance as she approached her blue minivan parked in the last slot in the third aisle from the street in front of the store.

She set the grocery bag down at her feet, holding the umbrella over herself and the bag as she juggled the key into the tip of the lock. *Darn!* No response. *What is going on here? Of all times for the lock to jam.*

Irene thought about calling her husband but realized she had left her cell phone at home in the charger. One bad episode after another had happened—and on a day when she was expecting company for lunch.

She felt like collapsing on the payment and sobbing—having a real pity party! She tried the key one more time. Still the lock wouldn't budge.

Suddenly someone came up behind her. She turned at the sound of a man's words. "Having a problem?" he asked. "Maybe I can help."

"Gee, thanks, but it seems the lock is jammed. I think I'll

need a locksmith for this one. I don't understand. This has never happened before!"

The gentleman smiled and produced a key as if by magic. "Try *this* one. I promise it will work." He chuckled as Irene stood there dumbfounded.

Then he pointed to a blue minivan one aisle over facing the same direction as the van she was standing next to. "And try your key in *that* vehicle!"

Irene put a hand to her mouth and burst out laughing. "You get the fairy godfather award for the day," she quipped. "I guess this is what my friends would call a 'senior moment.' Of course this is the *first* one I've ever had!"

The two nodded goodbye. Irene went off to *her* van, and the fairy godfather got into his.

Reflection

I will forget my complaint,
I will change my expression,
and smile (Job 9:27).

———————

Dear Lord, thank you for rescuing me from situations that appear overwhelming. They are nothing to you, but you never hold them over my head. You simply give me the grace I need without recrimination. How wonderful you are.

Running on Empty

"Have a nice weekend," Lettie called to her co-workers as they got out of Cathy's car and walked to their vehicles parked in the carpool lot.

"You too, Lettie," Cathy shouted just before she hit the accelerator and drove off. Lisa and Marion waved goodbye and went to their cars.

Lettie was parked at the far end of the lot, so she had a bit of a trek, but she didn't mind. "It felt good to move my legs and breathe the fresh air. As I got closer to the fence," she said, "I heard what I thought was an engine running. 'How odd,' I thought. 'I wonder where that sound is coming from? My car is the only one left in this area.' "

Then Lettie suddenly realized it *was* her car. *Oh no!* It had idled for nearly 12 hours, including travel time to and from Ohio State University, where all the women taught school.

"I stood there for a moment looking at my van as though an alien had descended on it," she said laughing. "The next thing I knew Marion and Lisa were beside me in their vehicles, asking if I needed help.

"I guess so," I said, feeling stupid. "I forgot to shut off the motor this morning. Can you believe it?" Then Lettie issued a stern warning. "Don't you dare breathe a word of this to my students, you rascals. They think I'm smart. I have a Ph.D.!"

The women roared as Lettie slid into the driver's seat and checked the fuel gauge. "Thankfully I filled my tank last night," she called out the window. "I think I have just enough to make it to the service station at the corner."

"Maybe one of us should follow you," said Lisa, "just in case..."

Lettie finished her sentence for her. "In case the old girl has lost all her marbles, leaves the car at the station, engine running, and then walks home! Okay, I'll take you up on it."

Lisa and Marion followed Lettie to the station. She filled her tank, then bought each of the gals a large soda. They stood in the driveway, clicked cans, and toasted the onset of mental-pause!

Reflection

My help comes from the LORD,
the Maker of heaven and earth (Psalm 121:2).

———————

How embarrassing to do something so contrary to my usual behavior. I'm shocked at some of the stunts I pull, O Lord. But you're not. You know I'm just a human being with all the failings and flaws that go with it. I'm so thankful that I can rely on you to help me work things out and recover my confidence.

Y Stop Now?

Jeanne is quick to admit, "I like maps with explicit directions—the kind I can get off the internet." Without this helpful tool she's at a loss, as was the case years ago *before* the internet provided everything from a recipe for homemade spaghetti sauce to a formula for raising foolproof African violets.

One weekend Jeanne was on her way to speak at a women's retreat at a conference center located deep in the woods. The meeting planner wrote out the directions by hand and mailed them to her in plenty of time.

> *Get on the retreat road by turning off the highway by the house with big butterflies on it. Then go a long way until you see the retreat sign.*

"I did go a long way," said Jeanne, "a *very* long way. Then the road split into a Y."

Now what? she wondered. There was no mention of a Y in the directions. The left part of the Y, with a few houses along its rim, looked more civilized than the right, so she chose that one.

"I looked for people along the way, or a store, or gas station—anything with live human beings who could help me out. But building after building was boarded up. I was beginning to think I had migrated to the Twilight Zone."

Jeanne kept going until the road narrowed, appeared muddy, and then rocky. "I could feel the hair on the back of my neck stand up. I knew I was in trouble. And to make matters worse, the sun had set and the woods were growing dark—fast."

Jeanne backed up to the beginning of the Y, turned around and headed back to where she had come from. *Surely someone else is in this part of the woods besides me. I hope so!* she thought.

Then suddenly around a curve came a carload of giddy women headed up the hill. Jeanne slammed on her brakes and flagged them with a white tissue she had pulled from her pocket.

They stopped and acknowledged they were on their way to the retreat too. "It's not far," said the driver. "Follow me."

Jeanne hugged their taillights, afraid to let them out of sight. Ahead she saw the famous Y come into view. The driver turned *right*. About one mile after that she turned *left* onto a rocky road that led to the rustic retreat site.

"I was never so happy to arrive anywhere in my life," said Jeanne. "Later I spoke with one of the participants, and she informed me that the year before she had taken the other road and wound up at the bottom of a gully by an abandoned logging camp!"

Jeanne thanked her for the chat and then went to bed, thinking about what she would share with the women the next day. "I had several talks planned, of course, but I knew I wanted to acknowledge what occurred since I learned a valuable lesson that day."

The following morning, Jeanne got up to speak after a time of worship, set aside her notes, and focused on a topic she had not planned—finding God's direction for our lives.

"I stressed the importance of listening and obeying the first time the Lord speaks," Jeanne shared. "Then we avoid the muddy ditches and rocky roads that lead us astray!"

Reflection

Direct me in the path of your commands,
for there I find delight (Psalm 119:35).

Lord, you know that I often go my own way and then come running to you when I mess up or get lost. Please help me today to hear your voice the first time and to follow the path you have set before me.

Shopping Spree

"Teresa? This is Mildred. I know you're going to the mall today. May I catch a ride with you?" Mildred shifted the phone to her good ear. "I'm not as comfortable driving in heavy traffic as I used to be. Pushing 80, you know," she added, reminding her younger neighbor of her advancing age.

"Of course," replied Teresa. "The kids and I will pick you up about eleven thirty, after Emily's morning nap."

"Thanks, Honey," said Mildred. "I'll walk out front as soon as I see you back out of the driveway."

Later that morning Teresa, Mildred, and the two children pulled up in front of Wal-Mart. Teresa helped Mildred out of the car and into the store. Mildred was going to look for sunglasses; Teresa was going to shop for children's clothing at the nearby Kids' Closet.

They agreed to meet at a certain time and location and then stop for lunch.

Mildred called Teresa on her cell phone when the young mother didn't show up as agreed. Then she paged her over the mall intercom system. Still no response. Finally, Mildred called a taxi and went home. She decided that being forgetful or hard of hearing were not traits exclusive to the elderly.

Late that afternoon, Mildred's phone rang as she was preparing dinner. It was Teresa calling.

"Mildred, I am so sorry. I just now realized I forgot to give you a ride home today. I feel so bad. What can I do to make up for it? I'm guessing not another ride!"

The two laughed. Then Mildred came up with an idea. "I hate eating alone," she said. "May I share a new dessert I made with you and your family?"

"We'd love it," said Teresa. "How about this? I'll make dinner; you bring dessert. Fortunately you won't need a ride to get here!"

Reflection

The Spirit helps us in our weakness (Romans 8:26).

Dear Lord, we all fall short when it comes to friendship. We misunderstand, overlook a need, say or do something we regret. Help me today to be mindful of the needs of others and to be conscientious about being a good friend.

Driving Miss Lucy

Lucy is the first to admit that she has great faith in God...and her driving attests to it. Well into her eighties, she is now required to take a driver's test each year in August. She begins praying about it in January. Her daughter Joan does not agree with her mother in prayer. Not that she wants to deny her mom's freedom, but Lucy's eyesight, hearing, sense of direction, and reflexes aren't the best anymore.

Lucy is sharp as a tack mentally, but also stubborn as a mule—according to Joan. "Before the required insurance and seat belt laws ten years ago, Mom at age 76, drove her 20-year-old Mustang 40 miles on the freeway to her dying sister's house every day for three years.

"We had plenty of arguments about her cruising with the semis in rush hour traffic, but to no avail. She'd shrug her shoulders, shake her pretty white-haired head, and comment, 'I say a prayer when I put my key in the door lock and the good Lord takes care of me!' "

But then Lucy was in an accident. However, that didn't stop her from looking ahead. "When are we going to shop for a new car?" she asked Joan from the gurney in the hospital where she was rushed after her collision.

"*Never!*" Joan replied emphatically.

"Okay. I forgot to wear my seat belt, and it was dark, and I didn't see the car coming at me. That's all. No biggie."

"*No biggie?*" Joan shouted. "Mom, you totaled three cars! Your Mustang literally took flight into a parked car which 'dominoed' into another parked car demolishing all three!"

"I don't know what you're talking about," said Lucy. "All I know is that I don't have a car! So when are we going to get one?"

"Mom, your driving days are over," Joan said after a long silence. "You're not going to get your license back. You had restrictions, remember? No driving at night, glasses required, and of course a seat belt at all times."

"How do you feel, ma'am?" the emergency room doctor asked Lucy.

"Fine, fine. Not a thing hurts! Just my poor car. Can you do anything about that?"

Reflection

Some trust in chariots and
some in horses, but we trust in the name
of the LORD, our God (Psalm 20:7).

Dear Lord, it's a challenge to give up our independence, especially when it comes to driving. We are so used to chauffeuring ourselves around town. How can we go back to buses and cabs and rides with friends and family when we long for the freedom to come and go as we wish when we wish? Help us to surrender peacefully and cooperatively when the time comes. With you at our side, we will be able to do all things in love—including giving up the wheel.

City Drivers

"Look at these New York drivers!" Pop bellowed as he drove down a familiar city street, chauffeuring his wife, Adele, and son Peter and his wife to a favorite restaurant. "They don't know the first thing about safe driving."

Peter sat in the rear seat, gripping the back of Pop's seat with white knuckles. "I had offered to drive, but he'd have none of it. He was proud of his new Buick, and he wanted to show it off— as well as prove to me that at age 81 he could still drive well."

"I don't see a problem," Peter remarked. "Seems like traffic is flowing nicely."

Pop turned to respond.

"Eyes on the road, please, Pop. I can hear you just fine," Peter said. He felt his pulse rise with his voice.

"Suddenly we were cruising faster than I thought the traffic could bear so I shouted, 'Pop, brakes! Quick! Can't you see how close you are to the car in front of you?'"

"Dang city drivers!" Pop shouted. "Why don't they slow down when it's time to stop instead of slamming on their brakes and blinding me with their red lights?"

Peter admits he should have left well enough alone, but he

took the bait, as usual, and fought for his point of view. "Look, Pop. Brakes protect us. They're to use in normal traffic and in fast stops when there isn't time to slow down gradually."

"You know how I feel about brakes. They're made to fail; that's what I think. Did I ever tell you about the time my brakes locked and…"

"Did he ever tell me? Only every time we were in the car together! I could practically recite the story word for word."

"Pop, that was 40 years ago," Peter reminded his father. "Cars are safer now. Brakes are tested…"

Peter didn't finish his sentence because there was Pop again, cruising along—so close this time that his son was certain they were going to tap the car in front of them.

Whew! Another close call, Peter thought.

Peter's father refuses to use his brakes except for an extreme emergency. And when he has used them, it's because he believes the other driver forced him into it.

"We arrived at our destination—a French cafe where we had planned a nice lunch," said Peter. "By the time we settled into our booth, I'd lost my appetite. After our meal, I noticed my father yawning. His eyes blinked. I knew it would be unsafe for him to drive."

"'Pop,' I asked, 'how about taking a snooze in the backseat while I drive us home? You deserve a *brake!*' "

"Very funny," Pop replied, but he took Peter up on the offer.

"We arrived home safe and sound," said Peter, letting out a long breath. "Then it was *my* turn to take a nap!"

Reflection

I will instruct you and teach you in the way you should go; I will counsel you and watch over you (Psalm 32:8).

Dear Lord, I can imagine that some of our shenanigans here on earth bring you a smile or maybe a cringe. Some things that are so important to us are so unimportant in the big picture—but you love us in spite of our pettiness and small worries. Thank you for doing so. I need every bit of love you have for me.

Bowled Over

Mimi walked out to the garage on Saturday morning to gather some gardening tools. She'd planned to work on her rose bed before it got too hot. Right away she realized she was out of fertilizer, so she jumped into her car to make the short jaunt to the gardening store in town.

She turned on the ignition but the wheels seemed locked. She couldn't go forward and she couldn't back up, yet the motor kept running. *How annoying!* she thought. Mimi finally had time to be outdoors and get a little sunshine and this had to happen. Did this mean she'd have to have the car towed to the dealership? What a pain.

Before calling for help, Mimi bent down and looked under the car. She wondered if something had broken off or if a branch or some strange object had gotten hung up. To her surprise there was a bowling ball lodged under the car. Her brother's bowling ball, engraved with his name! It must have rolled out of the storage cabinet when she opened the door to look for her tools. The slight forward slope of the garage floor was just the "alley" the ball needed. Had there been ten pins under the car, the ball would have scored a strike.

Mimi returned to the house and called out to Newt to pick up *his* ball that was lodged under *her* car. He gave her more than a funny look when she finished telling her tale. Sure enough she was right, as he found out when he looked under the car. Newt called a neighbor, who borrowed a jack from a friend down the street. Pretty soon men and women and kids were gathered in Mimi's garage to see the spectacle that had taken on a life of its own as people asked questions and then passed on the info to the next person they spoke with.

Finally, three men jacked up the car and the ball slid out and stopped at the wall. They all cheered, and then they went inside for coffee.

No gardening for Mimi that day! She'd had enough excitement for an entire week!

Reflection

Praise be to the God and Father of our
Lord Jesus Christ, the Father of compassion and
the God of all comfort (2 Corinthians 1:3).

———

Dear Lord, it is so comforting to know that even in the small, silly, incidental things you are there to rescue and comfort, to shield and guide. Thank you that nothing is too big or too small to catch your attention.

Par for the Car

Rhoda needed a new car, no two ways about it. This purchase would be the second one she made on her own, without the advice or assistance of a male relative or friend. She was a bit nervous at first, but then she tackled the job head-on.

"I searched the internet for reliable studies that listed makes and models that required the least maintenance, offered the best mileage, had strong safety features, and excellent performance and comfort," she explained. "I also read newspaper and magazine articles written by mechanics who excelled in their field of expertise."

Finally Rhoda selected the right car for her, bought it, and drove to the motor vehicle department to register it and get her new license plates.

"When it was my turn to speak with a clerk," said Rhoda, "the woman became overly solicitous. She saw that I was a senior and apparently thought I needed her to hold my hand!"

She walked Rhoda to the car, verified the vehicle number, then plied her with questions.

"Do you know how to raise the hood and insert the post to hold it up?

"Did anyone go with you when you bought the car?

"Are you confident you can drive and take care of the car in case of an emergency? I worry so about our older people being taken advantage of," she said in a tone one might use with a toddler.

Rhoda listened patiently and then answered concisely.

"Yes."

"No."

"Yes."

"Since you sound worried about me," said Rhoda in a confident tone, "let me add that I bought the car on my own after researching auto makes and models on the internet, downloading pages of information and studying them, visiting car dealerships, test driving, and grilling the salesperson before plunking down my money." *I guess I should tell her I prayed a lot too!*

The clerk looked at Rhoda with surprise and sudden respect. "It sounds like you did your homework," she said, "and you knew exactly what you were doing."

"Thanks. I feel good about it," Rhoda commented.

The clerk then turned toward the building, Rhoda at her side. "This may sound quirky," the woman added, "but I'm in the market for a new car myself, and...well, I wonder if I could impose on you to help me find the right one."

Reflection

I also saw under the sun this example of wisdom
that greatly impressed me (Ecclesiastes 9:13).

Lord, please help me to be a godly example in everything I do—from purchasing a car to sharing the truth of your Word with friends and strangers. Let my words be true and my actions without judgment.

Flat Wrong

G inny was suddenly aware of her car tugging to the right and then a loud flapping noise. "Oh no! A flat, I bet. What a time for this to happen. Lord, I don't know how to change a tire. I'll be late for work. I need help now!"

Just then she noticed a gas station at the next corner. Ginny managed to limp into the driveway and pull around to the repair shop. She phoned the office and told the receptionist about her dilemma. She promised to arrive as soon as possible following the repair.

"All set, Mrs. Moynihan," said the technician after inflating the tire. He backed her car out of the shop and onto the drive. "You'll be fine going to and from work, but you may need a new tire. I suggest you check the tires a couple of times over the next two days. If the tire gets soft again, come in and we'll fix you up with a new one."

Ginny thanked him and drove to work. At the end of the day she remembered to check the tire before starting home. She walked out to her gray station wagon and circled the car several times, inspecting each tire for any changes.

"Pardon me." An unfriendly voice caught her off-guard. "What on earth are you doing?"

Ginny continued her inspection without so much as a glance in the woman's direction. *Fat lot of nerve she has, asking what I'm doing to my own car,* she muttered silently. "If you must know," Ginny finally said, "I had a near-flat this morning, and the mechanic told me to check my tires before I drove home in case the tire deflated again. Now if you'll excuse me…"

"I can assure you, you won't find *your* flat tire here on *my* car!"

Ginny rose to her feet and slunk off to *her* gray station wagon—in the next aisle.

Reflection

Whoever listens to me will live in safety and be at ease, without fear of harm (Proverbs 1:33).

Dear Lord, before I'm so quick to judge another and get my feelings hurt, I ought to stop for a moment and see if my own actions and attitude need checking! Or I too risk being flat wrong.

Fast Getaway

Reena regretted that she never learned to drive, but at age 71 she wasn't about to take lessons. In one way she missed the independence that driving brings, but in another way she enjoyed having others drive her to the store, to doctors' appointments, and so on.

One Saturday morning her daughter's husband stopped by to fix a leaking pipe. While he was there, Reena asked if he'd mind driving her to the grocery store so she could stock up for the weekend.

"Be glad to," he said, "as soon as I'm finished."

An hour later the two were on their way, Brad behind the wheel of his pickup and Reena in the passenger seat, grocery list in hand.

He pulled into the parking lot of Shop 'n Save and Reena slid out. "Give me 20 minutes," she said. "I don't want to hold you up."

"No problem," Brad said. "I'll just put my head back and listen to the radio. Take your time."

Reena rushed around the market, plopping one item after another into her grocery cart. There was a long line at the check-out lane, and she worried about keeping Brad away from home too long.

Finally it was her turn. The checker rang up her items, Reena paid, and then hurried out the door. She rushed through the parking lot as quickly as she could while steering the cart with wobbly wheels. "Just my luck to get *this* one," she moaned.

She stopped for a moment to be sure she was going down the correct aisle. Then she spotted the white pickup and headed right to it. Reena plopped her bag into the cab in back and jumped in the passenger seat. She fastened the seat belt and turned to the driver. "Okay. Mission accomplished. Let's get out of here...oh my gosh, you're not Brad! Who are you?"

A huge grin broke across the driver's face. "I was going to ask you the same question! Where to? Sounds like you have something fun planned."

Reena was suddenly hot all over. She grabbed the door handle and popped out. "I'm so sorry," she called through the window. "Your truck looks just like my son-in-law's."

Just then Brad pulled up, laughing so hard he could hardly contain himself. "Going my way?" he shouted.

Reena reached for her bag of groceries, hoisted it out of the other man's cab, and held it tight as she slid into Brad's truck. Off they went, laughing all the way home.

Reflection

Then you will lift up your face without shame;
you will stand firm and without fear (Job 11:15).

———————————

Lord, these senior moments are becoming more and more embarrassing. I'm grateful I can hold up my head with you no matter what I do.

Creative Communicatin'

Remembering the Alamo!

Jonna and her friend Bertie and cousin Lena decided to take a break from their routine. All three had hit the big 50 and decided they were due for a celebration to kick off the next half-century of their lives. They planned a weekend getaway to Gatlinburg, Tennessee. After arriving and depositing their luggage at the bed-and-breakfast, they strolled the streets. As they came out of a souvenir shop, a car slowed down at the curb in front of the store. One of three young men inside leaned out the passenger window and called to the women.

"Where's the Alamo?" he shouted. "We're new here."

Jonna and Bertie chuckled. "These boys must be looped," Jonna commented.

"At the very least they need a history lesson," added Bertie.

The two moved to the side as Bertie stepped off the curb to answer their question.

"The Alamo is in Texas. Thataway," she added, pointing to the south.

The guy in the backseat called out his window. "Hey, pretty lady. Hop in. We'd sure appreciate it if you'd show us the way.

Right, boys?" He poked the driver in the arm and winked at the "girls."

"Sure thing. Plenty of room here for your girlfriends too. We can squeeze 'em in, no problem."

Bertie bantered a bit but then waved goodbye and wished them a good trip.

Later that day, the women jumped on the sightseeing trolley that would take them back to the parking lot where they had left their car.

"Oh no!" Lena shouted, as the driver turned down a side street. She burst out laughing. "Look, girls! There's the Alamo." She pointed to a building that appeared to be an exact replica of The Alamo in Texas! Above the building hung a big neon sign: Alamo Bar and Grill.

The women nearly fell off their seats laughing.

"Those boys must have thought *we* were looped," Jonna said.

"Let's just hope they spotted this place *before* heading for Texas," said Bertie.

Reflection

What advice you have offered
to one without wisdom! (Job 26:3).

Dear God, notice how I love to give advice even when I don't know what I'm talking about. Good thing you are here to remind me of my faults...and also to forgive them.

Candy Hearts

Nancy's husband, Jerry, knows her weakness for sweets. Every couple of weeks or so he brings home a box of caramel corn or toffee-covered pecans or a lemon meringue pie.

On Valentine's Day this year, Nancy awoke and stumbled into her office, sleep still in her eyes. She flipped on the computer and there next to her mouse was a small dish with several candy hearts, each with an encouraging phrase imprinted on it.

How thoughtful! she remarked to herself. "I popped a couple into my mouth, padded to the kitchen, plugged in the coffeemaker, and pulled out the frying pan," she said. "There on the counter were a few more hearts, so I shoved those into my mouth as well."

Nancy walked back to the bedroom, patted her face with a warm wet washcloth, and ran a brush through her tangled hair. "I leaned toward the mirror and on the shelf below it were three more candy hearts. *What the heck!* I thought. *It's Valentine's Day. Candy before breakfast is all right on such a special occasion.*"

Jerry came up behind Nancy and slid his arms around her waist. "Happy Valentine's Day," he chirped. "Did you like my surprise?"

"I love it. Thank you so much. You always knock me out when I least expect it. When did you plant all these hearts?"

"After you fell asleep," he said and kissed her on the neck. "How about some breakfast?"

"Meet you in the kitchen!"

Nancy cracked three eggs on the side of the skillet and dropped them into the melting butter. She opened the trash can to toss the eggshells and noticed a bunch of candy hearts.

"Jerry, what's this?" she asked, pointing to the discarded candies in the trash container. "Broken hearts?" she teased, pleased with her early morning banter.

"No. I tossed those, my love," he said, snuggling up to her in that romantic way of his, "because they didn't say what I wanted to express to you."

Nancy gulped, took her glasses out of the pocket of her bathrobe, and quickly put them on. She looked at Jerry, feeling a bit sheepish. "You mean I was supposed to *read* the candy hearts before I ate them?"

As Nancy recalled later, "So much for romance that day! I dished up the eggs then slid under the table in shame! Jerry joined me, and we had a good laugh and a Valentine's Day hug."

Reflection

Your love is more delightful than wine
(Song of Solomon 1:2).

Lord, I complain when I don't get enough attention from my spouse, and then I forget to acknowledge it when I do. My mate is a good person. I want to focus on the fruit, not the faults, in his/her life. Help me be encouraging so that our love will be sweet.

Green Jell-O

"Y ou lying piece of green Jell-O!" Raymond bellowed across the room to his wife, Paulette.

"*What* did you say?" Paulette barked, clearly insulted and confused.

Raymond looked at his wife like she'd lost her mind. Paulette popped off the sofa and ran out of the den in tears.

"What brought that on?" she asked God. "Is this it? Raymond is finally losing his mind? I know he's hard of hearing, but this is too much. What if he becomes dangerous?"

Paulette remembered having read about a man who chased his wife of 60 years out of the house with a butcher knife. He had been failing mentally for months, but then he became violent and she had to move him to a home for people with dementia. Paulette's thoughts raced on. Within seconds she was already planning what she'd tell their children and how their entire life would be turned upside down if Raymond were seriously mentally ill.

Paulette walked back to the den and stood in the doorway, ready to bolt if her husband lunged at her. She eyed him suspiciously. She knew it would only make matters worse if she got upset in front of him, so she controlled herself and asked him to repeat what he said. That would give her a chance to judge his mental state and decide what to do if he repeated the same phrase.

"You're lying on the cream pillow," he restated slowly in a loud voice.

Paulette burst out laughing. She and Raymond had agreed they would not rest their heads on the new cream-colored decorative pillows they'd bought for their sofa because they didn't want to stain them. Raymond was simply reminding her.

When she told him she thought he had called her a "lying piece of green Jell-O," he nearly fell off his chair laughing.

"After that my heart calmed down, and I let go of my fantasy of nursing homes and butcher knives," said Paulette.

"I'm not the only one around here who's hard of hearing!" exclaimed Raymond. "Looks like our next stop is the hearing aid center. I wonder if they have a two for the price of one sale?"

Reflection

Let me hear joy and gladness (Psalm 51:8).

Lord, thank you that even when I cannot hear you, you hear me and my cry for help. I pray today for the spiritual ears to hear your teachings and to apply them to my life.

Ma Bell

Judy and George looked at each other and sighed. "Mission accomplished," murmured George. "We did it—and it wasn't so bad after all."

The couple had committed to helping their 25-year-old son, Wes, move to his own apartment—the first time he'd lived apart from his parents. It was something of a milestone since Wes is schizophrenic and his odd habits can create stress for those around him. But the three had cooperated and now they stood back and reveled in the delightful new setting.

Wes had selected a comfortable sofa with matching chairs and a new television with a CD and DVD player built in. Judy surprised him with a comforter and plush pillows in his favorite shade of blue, and George had repainted the kitchen cabinets to complement the new countertops.

"A few weeks later we visited him," said Judy, "and our son Conrad joined us. He was amazed at what we had done and how well Wes was getting along on his own."

"If only Fred were here," George piped up as they sat down for a meal that Wes had prepared.

Just that fast Conrad's cell phone rang. "Con here," he said as he punched the connection key. Con mouthed the words everyone wanted to hear. "It's *Fred!*"

Judy jumped with happiness. What could be better? She and George and their three sons together, thanks to Ma Bell.

Fred was calling from Texas! *Lord, you must have told him to call. Couldn't be better timing,* Judy thought.

Suddenly any stress was transformed into joy. Everyone took a turn talking with Fred. Judy and George and their sons told jokes and recalled old times when the three boys had shared a single room so many years ago.

Now they're grown men, Lord, each with his own life. And George and I are visitors in their homes. Thank you for helping Wes over the hump—and for helping us too. We're all getting older...and definitely better!

Reflection

Your faith is growing more and more,
and the love every one of you has for each other
is increasing (2 Thessalonians 1:3).

Help me today, dear Jesus, to trust you in the difficulties and to praise you in the triumphs. I want to grow in grace and joy and gratitude. You are always there for me, no matter what.

Help Wanted!

illie walked into the banquet room and strode down the center aisle with confidence and enthusiasm. She had received the invitation to be the keynoter for the women's event nearly a year before. She had planned, prepared, and prayed for this moment for months. It was finally her turn to inspire the audience with a message she felt passionate about. All her notes were in order and her props already on the table beside the microphone.

She strode to the lectern, and the women applauded before she uttered a word. Billie was stunned by this amazing show of appreciation. She opened her talk with a joke to break the ice and then moved right in to her presentation about the value of friends as we age.

"I remember my mother telling me that friends at any age are precious, but they become even more of a treasure when you get older, knowing your time together is growing short."

Billie felt encouraged by women nodding in agreement, and she felt vulnerable to the topic herself since her best friend had recently been diagnosed with breast cancer. Her eyes flooded with tears and her voice caught. "My goodness!" she exclaimed.

"I had no idea I was going to have such a response. I'm realizing right now how dear to me my own friends are.

"I remember being impacted by a beautiful quotation from Mary Kay...Mary Kay...Oh, who am I trying to think of? Somebody help me, please," she said, suddenly falling prey to a senior moment. "The woman who started the famous makeup company."

The audience tittered as Billie suddenly realized what she'd said. "I've got it!" she said laughing and pressing her hand to her mouth. "Mary Kay Ash, of course. Well, there you go. I'm proving my point, aren't I? I need friends as I age and here you are. Thank you."

This was the perfect unplanned example. Billie finished her talk, and the women jumped to their feet in a standing ovation.

Reflection

If one falls down, his friend
can help him up (Ecclesiastes 4:10).

Thank you, Lord, for friends and companions who offer me a hand when I need it, comfort when I'm sad, and a word of encouragement when I mess up. But most of all, thank you for calling me a friend of yours.

Nice Game

Nora and Larry were proud of their grandson, Phil. He had made the college basketball team, as did his childhood friend, Roy. Nora looked forward to attending the playoffs with both young men on the court.

"I wanted to make a good impression on Phil and his friends, to show them that I was a hip grandma, still attractive for my age, and that I knew a thing or two about athletics," said Nora.

So she spent the afternoon before the game in the hair salon. "I had a facial, a wash and blow dry, and a manicure and pedicure. I wore my new Calvin Klein jeans and a cute striped shirt. The only thing missing to make the look complete was a stylish pair of glasses frames. Unfortunately, my new lenses and frames wouldn't be ready till the following week, and I was not about to wear the ugly specs I was trading in. I decided I would make do. We had front-row seats and my husband would be with me, so he could fill me in on any plays too far away for me to see clearly."

As the couple drove to the game, Larry briefed Nora *again* on the nuances of basketball and reminded her of who was who on the team. He knew the numbers of all the players.

"The game was a thriller, I have to admit," Nora said later. "Phil and his team played hard and won hard! After the game, Larry and I rushed to the court with hundreds of screaming fans.

"Phil, we are so proud of you!" Nora squealed and threw her arms around her six-foot-four grandson.

His teammate Roy stood beside him. "You too, Roy," Nora said and reached up to hug him. "I'm just so proud of the two of you."

"Thanks, Grams," said Phil. Then he turned to Roy and shrugged.

Roy chuckled and hugged Nora back. "Thank you, Mrs. Johnson, but I haven't played since last year. You probably missed seeing me on the bench."

Nora's face grew hot with embarrassment! "Oh...but you played great last year," she blurted out without thinking, then excused herself to go to the ladies' room. "I needed a good splash of cold water!"

Reflection

You are my hiding place;
you will protect me from trouble
and surround me with
songs of deliverance (Psalm 32:7).

Sometimes, Lord, I embarrass myself to the point of wanting to hide! But then I remember that you are my hiding place and you will always guide me back to right thinking and behaving.

Souvenirs

onnie, her husband, Mike, and their two grandsons, Jamie and Richey, drove to Southern California from their home in the northern part of the state. The boys were eager to visit the San Diego Zoo and to ride the waterslide at Sea World.

Bonnie had packed a lunch of cold cuts, crackers, sliced bread, pickles, tomato slices, chips, and chocolate chip cookies.

Mike was concerned about the cooler. He was sure it was on the fritz and no longer able to keep the perishables cold enough. Bonnie pooh-poohed his notion. "It's good enough," she said. "We'll be stopping to eat by noon. Nothing will spoil that quickly."

"All right," he countered, winking at his wife at the same time. "But if someone gets sick it will be on your head."

Bonnie saluted. "Aye, aye, sir. I accept full responsibility."

Off they went, the boys busy with computer games, Bonnie and Mike enjoying the scenery as they passed through various towns along the coast on their way south.

They stopped for a bathroom break in the town of Santa Nella. One of the boys piped up from the backseat, "Look at the sign, Grandpa: Santa Nella Souvenirs. Can we get one here? Puleeze!"

Grandpa Mike swung over to the shoulder of the road, pulled on the emergency lights, and turned to the boys. "Salmonella! Who has salmonella?" Then he drilled his wife with his eyes. "I told you the cooler didn't work."

Bonnie reached for her husband's hand and spoke directly into his good ear. "No one has salmonella," she said sweetly. "Santa Nella, honey, a place for souvenirs. The boys want to stop there."

Mike took his wife's response good-naturedly. Then he came back with a line of his own. "Do you suppose I can get a souvenir there too? Hearing aids!"

Everyone laughed as Grandpa Mike pulled off at the next exit and headed for Santa Nella Souvenirs.

Reflection

Consequently, faith comes from
hearing the message, and the message is heard
through the word of Christ (Romans 10:17).

———————

Dear Lord, I find it interesting that I hear what I want to hear and don't hear what I don't want to hear. And sometimes I hear the worst! Please make me sensitive to hearing you above all.

Hallmark of Confusion

Rosalie started a unique ministry. She sends greeting cards to various friends and neighbors for a variety of occasions—from birthday wishes to condolences on the death of a loved one. And just for fun she sends cards for everything from Grandparents' Day to Groundhog Day. The more unusual ones, such as Friendship Day (first Sunday in August), Stepfamily Day (September 16), and Native American Day (fourth Friday in September) catch the attention of many of her friends.

Rosalie's calendar keeps her up-to-date on the well-known and lesser-known holidays. And Hallmark and American Greeting Cards provide a wide range of choices when she's shopping for the latest bunch of cards or she makes her own.

This hobby and ministry is not as simple as it appears. One can get confused trying to keep up with all the opportunities that call for a thoughtful card and note. Rosalie is thinking of engaging a capable assistant to help her keep track of who received what, when, and why. That day may arrive sooner than later, based on what occurred recently.

Rosalie chose a card for a woman in her neighborhood who had given birth to a baby boy. That same day she picked out one for a 94-year-old man who was recovering from surgery on his right arm. She wrote a personal note to each, signed the cards, and popped them into the mail on Thursday morning. On Sunday after church, the young mother approached Rosalie and thanked her for her thoughtfulness. Then she chuckled.

"I did have some pretty intense labor pains," she admitted, "but it didn't result in arm surgery."

Rosalie put a hand to her mouth in embarrassment. "Oh, no, I put my friend John's card in your envelope. How silly of me."

The two women had a good laugh. Then Rosalie remarked, "Can you imagine how surprised John must have been to receive a card congratulating him on his newborn son?"

Reflection

May the words of my mouth and
the meditation of my heart
be pleasing in your sight, O Lord,
my Rock and my Redeemer (Psalm 19:14).

Lord, thank you for the gift of laughter. I want to be able to smile when I make an honest mistake, knowing you're right there to pick me up and laugh with me.

Unruly E-Mail

Roger booted up his computer, reached for the cup of coffee on his desk, and sipped the strong brew while waiting for his e-mail program to open. He looked at his calendar and then at the clock on the wall. Too much to do in too little time. He felt overwhelmed.

"Something's gotta give," he mumbled to himself as he watched more than 100 e-mails tumble onto the screen. He counted three pitches for a new mortgage, four come-ons for Rolex look-alikes, and at least half a dozen lures to purchase Viagra. He continued to scroll and delete until he finally landed on a legitimate message from one of his female colleagues.

> *Roger, quick note to remind you we are meeting after work Thursday at 5:00 in my office to discuss quarterly goals. Please be prompt. I have another meeting at 6:00, and we have a lot to cover in one hour.*
>
> *See you then.*
>
> *Paulette*

Roger checked his daily planner and scribbled in the time and purpose for the meeting. Then he hit REPLY and typed in a response to Paulette.

> *Paulette, got your memo. Count on me to be there. Indecently, I'll arrive on time for a change. I know you'll be happy to hear that.*
>
> *Roger*

Roger hit SEND and within a moment an IM came through from Paulette.

> *Roger, give me that again. You'll arrive* inde-cently? *No, I'm not happy to hear that.*
>
> *Paulette*

Roger felt his face grow hot with embarrassment. He rechecked his message to Paulette. Sure enough he had typed in the word *indecently* when he had meant to say, *incidentally*. He apologized for the error—promptly and with decency!

Reflection

Let us behave decently, as in the daytime (Romans 13:13).

Lord, I feel stupid when I make such embarrassing mistakes, but I'm blessed to know you never hold them against me. You have paid the price for all my sins...and for my bloopers too!

Pinch-hit Mother

Glenna was getting older, so of course she knew her mother wouldn't be with her much longer. Still, she didn't want to face the reality of losing her until she absolutely had to.

"My husband and I were in Spain, visiting our younger daughter and her family who are missionaries. One morning everyone had gone out to run errands, and I had agreed to stay behind to take care of three-year-old Megan and her baby sister."

The phone rang. Glenna answered it and recognized the voice of her older daughter, Tara. "Brace your heart, Mom," she said, half-sobbing. "Grammy died in her sleep last night."

Taken by surprise, Glenna was clearly shaken. Her mother had not seemed critically ill when she left her just two weeks before. Glenna listened to Tara explain the details. Her mind reeled as she tried to think of what she could do from so far away.

Little Megan was standing near the phone, taking in what she heard. Of course she was concerned when she saw her grandmother burst into tears. At that moment, sweet Megan gently placed her hands in her grandmother's. "Why are you crying, Grammy?" she asked.

Glenna bent down to explain in words she hoped Megan could understand. "Because my mother has just gone to heaven," she said, trying to control her tears.

"Megan looked at me with her soft blue eyes and did her best to console me."

"Don't cry, Grammy," she said with complete confidence. "We'll get you another mother."

Her concerned smile and tender words turned Glenna's sorrow into laughter.

Reflection

Cast your cares on the LORD and
he will sustain you (Psalm 55:22).

Dear Lord, in times of trial and difficulty the tender words of a young child can be such a healing balm. I am reminded that I must be as a little child myself in order to enter your kingdom when my time on earth is finished.

Heavenly Hotel

"Laura, Mitch, come here, please." Iris called her son and daughter-in-law to her bedside in the nursing home. "Pretty soon I'll be gone, and I want to be sure you know my wishes before I go."

Mitch patted his mother's soft hand. "Mom, you can relax. Laura and I have everything written down. I promise we'll take care of all the details exactly the way you want us to. Please relax."

He glanced at the wall over his mother's bed. It was filled with framed acknowledgments of her many accomplishments over the 94 years of her life. She had completed college—the first in her family of seven siblings to do so—and had gone on for a master's degree in education. She had served as the president of the Women's Auxiliary at the local hospital, and one year had been voted Volunteer of the Year for spearheading a reading program for underprivileged children.

"Mom, you've done it all, and you were a great mother, as well. We love you." Mitch leaned over and kissed her frail face. He felt tears well in his eyes as he realized any visit could be his last.

Iris was not one for sentiment, so she went back to her list of do's and don'ts for her funeral. Mitch snapped to attention as he repeated her wishes.

"I have a lot of friends here in Phoenix, some are gone, but there are still plenty, so have the funeral here in town. Then ship my body to Minneapolis where Hal and Ben are buried. I want to be in the same plot with my two husbands. Bless their souls, I wonder what they'd think of sharing me! Guess we'll never know." She laughed at the thought.

Iris sat forward and looked first at Mitch and then at Laura. "Listen carefully, please. Now, when we arrive in Minnesota for the second funeral service, I'll stay with the Petersons and you and your family will be in a motel. Might be wise to decide now where you want to stay so you won't be stuck at the last moment."

Laura looked at Mitch. They both grinned. "Mother, one nice thing about it being *your* funeral, you won't have to stay with the Petersons or worry about where we stay," said Laura.

Iris laughed out loud as she realized what she'd said. "Oh my, you're right, Laura! I'll be staying with Jesus. He said he's preparing a place for me."

"Right, Mom, and it will be perfect."

Reflection

Come, you who are blessed by my Father;
take your inheritance, the kingdom
prepared for you since the creation
of the world (Matthew 25:34).

Lord, I get excited thinking about the place you've prepared for me when I am taken to heaven to spend eternity with you. But in the meantime, while I'm still here on earth, help me to be faithful in following your commands and in reaching others with your love and provision.

Oopsy!

"I remember the day I rushed my mother to the hospital with a bleeding ulcer," said Sarah. "She was about to celebrate her eighty-eighth birthday. Now it appeared she'd spend it and several more days in the hospital. I needed to change plans fast. Cancel—no postpone—the party I had planned for her. Call my sister, Candace, in New York and tell her what was going on. Get hold of my two brothers, one in Germany on business and one on vacation in the Bahamas."

Sarah felt as though everything fell on her since she was the one sibling who lived in the same town as their mother. She pulled out her phone book, jotted down some numbers, turned on the computer, and brought up her e-mail program.

"My hands shook," recalled Sarah. *What if I lose Mom before my sister and brothers arrive?* she thought. *A bleeding ulcer is serious for anyone, but for an 88-year-old woman it could be fatal.* Her mind raced ahead to funeral arrangements, interment, food following the service. "I was a wreck. I couldn't think straight. Mom had told me where she kept everything— just in case—but now my mind was blank. I couldn't remember a thing she had said."

Then Sarah realized Candace might know where everything was. *I'll call her first. No I'll e-mail her. That way she won't hear the worry in my voice,* she decided.

Sarah began typing as fast as she could: "Candy, no cause for alarm, but Mom's in the hospital with a bleeding ulcer. We may need to postpone the party, but not for long. And don't worry. I have everything under control. I've ordered an autopsy—just to be sure. Love, Sarah."

She pushed SEND and sat back to breathe.

Ding! The sound of an IM startled her to reality.

"Sarah, I think you mean *biopsy,* not *autopsy!* Stay right where you are. I'm catching the next flight. Love, Candy."

Reflection

Have no fear of sudden disaster (Proverbs 3:25).

God, I know that you know what is ahead for me and for every member of my family. You have all the details worked out. When I trust you, I am not afraid. When I rely on my own strength, I panic. Please help me today to turn over all my cares and worries and to rest in the assurance of your everlasting direction and peace.

Lip Glue

Ellie's daily routine is filled with bags and baskets. She has a canvas bag for magazines she plans to read. Another bag contains notepaper, pens, envelopes, and stamps for the occasional thank-you note or letter she enjoys writing. There's a bag for knitting supplies, and one with needle, thread, assorted buttons, and small scissors for a bit of mending.

Her various baskets each have a purpose as well. And she carries one with her whenever she goes outside to garden, to pick flowers, to prune a stray twig or vine, or to even enjoy a lunch or a snack on her sunlit patio.

"One of the advantages," she claims, "is that I rarely misplace anything. When I'm ready for a chore or task, I go to my basket shelf or to the closet where I hang my bags. One quick look and I have what I need. I also make a point of returning the items I use to the appropriate container."

One such basket contains a glue stick, pens, highlighters, scissors, paper clips, White-Out, and ChapStick, suitable for a variety of spontaneous tasks or needs. "Several weeks ago," said Ellie, "I grabbed that particular basket to take out to my porch to enjoy a bit of sunshine."

She had just written a letter and was about to seal the envelope when she discovered the glue on the inside flap had dried out. It wouldn't stick. *No problem*, thought Ellie. *I can use the glue stick*. She reached into her basket for the item, feeling clever about having just what she needed at her fingertips.

"After a heavy application of the stick," said Ellie, "I was annoyed the envelope flap still would not stick. It popped back up the moment I pressed it down."

Good heavens! I thought. *They don't even make glue sticks the way they used to. I should take it back and ask for a refund.*

She checked the brand and suddenly realized, "It's ChapStick, not a glue stick." Ellie had a good laugh and sighed in relief. "Imagine where'd I be right now if I had applied glue stick to my chapped lips. I'd be in the emergency room at the hospital using sign language to communicate!"

Reflection

Is there any wickedness on my lips?
Can my mouth not discern malice? (Job 6:30).

———————————

Lord, I cannot praise you with my lips sealed tight. I have to open them in order to speak my praise and gratitude for rescuing me from my own forgetfulness. You are always here for me in everything I think, say, and do. May I also be with you in each of those moments.

Don't Try That Again!

Priority Mail

Steve woke up with a start. Mindy wagged her tail and licked his face. She was ready for their morning walk. Steve staggered out of bed, rubbed the sleep from his eyes, and splashed cold water on his face. He pulled on his sweats and running shoes and reached for Mindy's leash.

"Calm down, girl. It's okay. We're going, don't worry. I had a late night, remember?"

Steve grabbed a plastic bag and scooper from the cabinet under the kitchen sink. He was always careful to clean up after his pup. All the dog owners on his block were respectful of each other's property.

As they passed through the front hall, Steve noticed a stack of stamped envelopes on the bench by the door. *Might as well mail these bills while we're out,* he thought.

The two set out and headed for the park, Mindy's favorite spot. She strained on the leash as she sniffed the grass and flowers and searched out just the right place to take care of her morning business.

Steve remembered the mailbox on the corner of Dana Drive and Fourth Street. He coached Mindy in that direction so he could drop off the bills. With the leash and envelopes in one hand and the doggie bag in the other, they trotted across the street and down the block. Steve paused at the box, dropped his stash in the opening, and then headed down Dana Drive toward home. It had been a good morning. Mindy was happy. And Steve felt refreshed. He was eager for that first cup of coffee and a couple of poached eggs on toast.

Mindy made the most of the last couple of blocks. She sniffed and relieved herself a few more times, then tugged at the leash as they rounded the corner near home.

Steve pushed open the front door and noticed he was still holding the stamped envelopes. "What? I could have sworn I mailed...*Oh no!* I mailed the poop! That poor mail carrier!"

Then he roared laughing. "I wonder if it will come back for insufficient postage? I guess not since I (thank goodness!) forgot to add a return address sticker!"

Reflection

As the Scripture says,
"Anyone who trusts in him
will never be put to shame"
(Romans 10:11).

God, some days I wake up feeling excited and eager for what's ahead and then boom!—something happens to throw me off. Often it's because of my own foolishness or the foolishness of others. Please help me today to focus on you, to trust and obey, to put all my cares aside, and to know that even when I mess up you are there to help me clean it up.

Coffee Anyone?

Anita walked into the kitchen, her mind a whirl of thoughts. Her guests would arrive for brunch at any moment. The blueberry scones were cooling on the counter next to the oven. The chocolate-tipped strawberries looked beautiful on the glass plate. Sugar and cream, spoons, plates, and napkins were laid out on the serving bar. And the spinach quiche would be ready to slice at any moment.

What else? Anita knew there was one more thing to do before Leonard and Margaret walked through the front door. *But what is it?* she pondered.

The door chime pierced her thoughts, and she ran to answer it. She welcomed her friends and motioned them into the family room. "I'm thrilled you could come," she said, kissing Margaret on the cheek and hugging Leonard. "Dan will be home in a sec. He's running an errand."

Anita carried on, making small talk while Margaret and Leonard filled in the empty spots with news of their kids, grandchildren, and travel. Anita made the right sounds and facial expressions, but her mind was searching for the one task left to do. She couldn't remember it for the life of her.

Leonard held up an empty cup. "Coffee ready yet?" he asked. "I missed my usual this morning."

"Of course." Anita reached for the pot, and then suddenly realized the missing item on her to-do list: *Coffee!* "I'm sorry. I forgot to make it. It'll just be a minute. So tell me about your cruise to Alaska," she said as all three of them moved into the kitchen.

Anita filled the coffeepot with water as they talked, placed it on the burner plate, and poured fresh-ground coffee into the filter. She flipped the switch to ON and continued talking. After a moment she heard a weird popping sound. Leonard pointed to the pot.

"I think you forgot to pour the water into the coffeemaker."

Anita could see he was stifling a grin.

"Of course," she said, feeling her neck turn as red as the strawberries on the plate. Quickly she poured the pot of water into the container and let out a long breath.

"Now to heat some water for tea," she joked. "I think I'll trust the microwave with that job."

An hour later Anita and Dan and Margaret and Leonard were finishing the last of the blueberry scones and the chocolate-tipped strawberries. There was only one slice of quiche remaining and the coffeepot was now empty.

"Delicious coffee blend," Leonard remarked. "It was worth waiting for!"

Anita caught the glint in his eye. "I'll let you in on a little secret," she said. "You start with water in the pot on the burner plate and when you hear a popping sound you pour the water into the coffeemaker—where it should have gone in the first place!"

Reflection

My help comes from the LORD,
the Maker of heaven and earth (Psalm 121:2).

How embarrassed I feel when I make silly mistakes. My face flushes and my palms perspire. I want to run and hide. I hate it when I make a fool of myself. But you remind me over and over in your Word that my help and my refuge are in you. Oh Lord, today help me remember that and to live in that promise.

Melon Mania

"A nything else?" Bob called from the car.

Maria looked up from the flowerbed. "No, just the things on the list. Thanks a million."

Bob drove off and ten minutes later pulled into the parking lot in front of Save-a-Lot. As he approached the front of the store, he noticed a tall box of watermelons on a pallet. Watermelon was not on the shopping list, but this group looked good—and they were only $2.99 apiece.

Bob bent over the box to search for the perfect size. He couldn't reach the one he wanted, so he stepped into the box and leaned down to pick it up. As he stood up he butted heads with a woman who was leaning over the other side of the box.

"Pardon me," he said. Bob's face flushed and the woman stepped back in surprise. They both laughed. "I'm so sorry. You probably think I just fell off the watermelon truck," he joked.

"No harm done," she said. "Have a nice day."

"You too," Bob said as he stepped out of the box, tripped on the edge of the pallet, dropped the melon, and landed on top of it. The rind burst open! Pulp, juice, and seeds sprayed everything in sight! Bob stood up and looked down at his shirt. It was wet and sticky from neckline to beltline.

Maybe not a truck. But I did just fall out of a watermelon box! he thought as he grinned.

The store manager strode forward, roped off the section by the box, and ordered one of the bag boys to start cleaning up the mess.

Bob took a deep breath, brushed the seeds from his hair, and stepped over the rope. People gathered around, staring and chuckling.

Lord, I feel like a sideshow at a circus, Bob decided. Another employee rushed to the scene with a hose and brush. Gradually the gawkers dispersed.

The manager stepped forward. "Sir, what can I do to help? I'm sorry about this unfortunate…"

Bob interrupted. "I'm fine. It's my fault, not yours," he said and shook the man's hand. "If I had stuck to the list my wife gave me, none of this would have happened."

"Have a watermelon on us," said the manager.

Bob winked. "Thanks, but I already had one on you. Now it's *on* me."

Bob pulled himself together and swiped at his shirt with a handkerchief. No real harm done—except to the melon! He felt embarrassed and a bit stupid too, but he was all right. He could have broken a bone or sprained his foot. He whispered a prayer of thanks and walked to his car.

Reflection

The Lord knows how to
rescue godly men from trials (2 Peter 2:9).

If it weren't for your love and mercy, I'd be down all the time—and with a lot more than watermelon juice and a few seeds on my shirt. But you chose to rescue me from sin and shame, not because of anything I did but because of what Jesus did for me on the Cross.

Thank you.

Spell It Again, Sam

Corey walked up and down the aisles of the supermarket, selecting one item after another. A box of cereal. A bottle of apple juice. A dozen eggs. Two cans of cream of mushroom soup. A couple of ripe tomatoes and a sack of Idaho potatoes. "That should do it," she muttered to herself. As she passed by the freezer foods, she caught her reflection in the glass doors, then gasped. "Lord, I hope I don't run into anyone I know! I can't get by in public anymore without makeup. I really should take time to look nice before leaving the house!"

So far so good, she thought as she wheeled the cart to the checkout stand and unloaded her groceries onto the conveyor. Two check stands over, she spotted a familiar face. *Janice, no Jody...or is it Jean? That doesn't sound right either. What is her name? If I could think of her last name, I'm sure her first name would pop up. Here I go again. Names are dropping from my mind as fast as leaves from a tree in autumn.*

Corey didn't want to embarrass herself, especially considering the way she looked in her painter's shorts and faded T-shirt and with her hair pushed on top of her head with a clip that didn't quite do the job.

I'll look the other way. Hey, there's nothing to worry about. She won't recognize me in this get-up. I'll pay and go—fast. Corey was pleased with her plan.

"Corey, hi! I thought it was you I spotted." The woman hurried over and reached out for a hug. "It's been a couple of years at least. Do you live around here?"

God, please, what is her name? I'd rather die than admit I don't know it. Look at how friendly she is. How embarrassing to have to ask her name.

"So what's new with you and Gene?" the woman probed as Corey handed the clerk her charge card and then signed the receipt.

She not only remembers me, but my husband too? Oh great. This is getting worse by the minute.

"Gene. Yes, Gene's fine. And you and your family?" *I don't remember if she's married or has children. This is awful.*

Corey pushed her basket through the stand and headed for the door, turning to the woman, while still fishing for her name.

"I'm alone now," the woman said. "Skip died last year. It's been quite an adjustment."

"I'm sorry..." Corey said, uncertain about what to say next.

"Maybe we can get together," the woman said. "I'm doing my best to reconnect with old friends. It's a blessing to run into you."

Corey felt her palms grow wet and her heart race. She gathered all the courage she could muster. "Help me out, will you? I seem to remember..." Corey lost her nerve. She just couldn't admit that she had forgotten the woman's name.

"As I recall," she stammered, "your name has an unusual spelling. Would you mind telling me again? I want to get it right once and for all."

"Jill. J-I-L-L. Jones. J-O-N-E-S."

And now for my next act! Corey said to herself as she cringed.

Reflection

Those who complain
will accept instruction (Isaiah 29:24).

Dear God, my "rememberer" isn't working too well these days, especially with names from the past. I need some help. Mostly I need your grace to give up being too proud to ask for help when I need it. There's no shame in forgetting. But there is shame in not acknowledging that I'm human and can use a bit of assistance from time to time.

Fe-Fi-Fo-Film

Harriet and Ralph stopped in front of the monkey enclosure. "Look!" shouted Harriet. "They are so cute. I can't believe their antics. They're just like us—well, almost! I can't swing from branch to branch anymore, but I can peel a banana with the best of the bunch, pun intended!" She elbowed her husband in the ribs. It took him awhile to get her humor—like about 55 years of marriage.

Oh well, she thought. *He has talents I don't have, like taking pictures and knowing how to download them on the computer and create albums I can send to our kids and grandkids.*

"Ralph, quick! Snap one of that darling baby and its doting mother. I want to send it to Kelly. You know how she's always had a thing for monkeys ever since she was a little girl."

Harriet moved closer to Ralph. She stood right in front of him, but he didn't budge. "Are you all right?" she asked, worried that he had zoned out completely and she'd have to call for help.

Ralph batted her away with his left hand as he examined the camera in his right. Then he pushed buttons, opened and closed the shutter, looked through the lens, focused and snapped. Nothing!

"It's jammed," he bellowed. "Darn thing isn't worth the

metal it's made of. What's happening to manufacturers these days? They can't get it right. Just when I'm about to shoot a roll the whole thing locks up."

He paced back and forth in front of the enclosure, fuming and muttering. Harriet slumped against the fence, feeling exasperated and disappointed. She had so looked forward to this day at the zoo. Now it was spoiled. They wouldn't have even one souvenir picture to share with friends and family.

"I know," she said, brightening. "We'll buy a pack of postcard photos in the gift shop. It's the next best thing."

Ralph was not so easily pacified. He was mad! Good and mad. He yanked the strap off his neck just as a young man with two small children walked over to him.

"Excuse me, sir. Maybe I can help. I overheard you saying your camera is on the fritz and it's brand-new. I'll be happy to take a look. Cameras can be a bit confusing."

He took the camera from Ralph, looked through the lens, and returned it with a smile. "Simple remedy," he said. "Load a roll of film, and you'll be in business. Have fun!"

Harriet watched her husband's face go from pink to red as he eked out a "thank you," then hurried down the walkway.

"Wait for me," she called. "I have an extra roll in my purse."

Reflection

A quick-tempered man
does foolish things (Proverbs 14:17).

Dear God, being impatient gets me every time. I'm ready to blame others when I'm the cause of my own upset. Help me to turn to you for comfort and guidance when I'm frustrated instead of taking out my feelings on someone I love.

Sweet Somethings

Breakfast Bonanza

Roger parked his van in the driveway of his parents' house. His sons, eight-year-old Jason and four-year-old Wally, tugged at their duffels and sleeping bags stuffed into the back of the car. They hopped out of the car and ran up the walkway. Their dad grabbed them just before they rang the bell.

"Remember, boys, this is a *treat*. Grandma and Grandpa aren't as young as they used to be. Be on your best behavior, all right? No fussing when Grandma says it's bedtime, and you eat everything on your plate, you hear? Make your mom and me proud."

"We will, Dad, I promise," said Jason.

"Me too," echoed Wally.

The boys tore away from their dad when the door opened and Grandma and Grandpa spread their arms wide to greet them.

Roger hugged his parents and thanked them for taking the boys. "I've had a good talk with Jason and Wally. They know what I expect of them. I'll be looking for a clean report. Don't be afraid to discipline if needed."

"Roger, you and Jan go on now and have a good time. We

raised you, and you turned out all right. I think we can handle two little boys for a weekend."

"'Thanks," he said and hugged his sons and waved good-bye.

On Sunday afternoon Roger returned to pick up the boys. He was happy to hear they had gone to Sunday school and had eaten a hearty brunch. He picked up Wally and wiped off the crumbs from his mouth. "What'd you have, Little Buddy? Smells good in here."

Jason stepped in and answered for his younger brother. "We had calcium, protein, and fruit," he said proudly.

"Mom, what's this all about? Did you give them a lesson in basic nutrition?"

Roger walked into the kitchen and there on the counter was the evidence—a carton of ice cream, two banana peels, a package of crushed nuts, a squeeze bottle of chocolate syrup, and a jar of maraschino cherries!

"Grandma made us banana splits!" Wally volunteered.

"And we ate everything she put on our plates," said Jason, "just like you told us to, Dad."

Roger started to say something to his mother and then paused. "Sounds good to me," he said, winking at the boys. "Mom, got any calcium, protein, and fruit left over for *your* son?"

Reflection

You will have plenty to eat,
until you are full, and you will praise
the name of the LORD your God (Joel 2:26).

Lord, thank you for treats, for fun, for good times with family and friends. You never disappoint me. You not only provide for my needs, but you are my very portion.

Knit One, Purl Two

Knitting needles. Check.
Potting soil. Check.
Swimsuit and cap. Check.
Scrabble game. Check.
Journal. Check.
Camera. Check.

Leslie laid the list of items on the kitchen counter. She chuckled at the diversity. "I've learned to knit, swim, journal, take photos, and grow African violets—and I can play a pretty fair game of Scrabble too. Not bad for a 'little old lady,' or LOL, as my grandchildren refer to me."

She thought back over the years and realized her way of handling crises was to take up a new hobby. When she looked at the list again, she laughed out loud. *According to this, my life's been a mess!* But then she realized that God had given her a beautiful gift—a talent for turning clouds inside out, for using her mind and heart for good instead of dwelling on the difficult and murmuring about the impossible.

The sound of the phone interrupted her thoughts.

"Mom, Pat here. Jenna and I are going to the beach this

afternoon. Want to join us? A swim sounds like a perfect solution to this muggy weather."

Leslie felt her heart pound at the sound of her daughter's voice. Pat had been distant for no apparent reason for the past month. She hadn't returned phone calls and she... *What does it matter? She's calling now. Focus on that,* Leslie told herself.

"Sure, count me in," she responded. "What can I bring? Snacks, drinks, cookies? Beach blankets?"

"I've got the food covered, and Jenna has an extra blanket. But if you really want to contribute something..." Pat hesitated. "Probably sounds crazy, Mom, but Jenna and I want to learn to knit. Think you could show us the basics? We're going through some tough times, and we need something to help us cope. I'll tell you more when I see you."

Leslie smiled heavenward. *Lord, you have some pretty unique ways of resolving problems and bringing loved ones together. Who'd have imagined that next to my Bible, my knitting needles would be an answer to prayer?*

Reflection

He stilled the storm to a whisper;
the waves of the sea were hushed (Psalm 107:29).

God, thank you for knitting me to you and others when there are misunderstandings. When I focus on you instead of the problem, all is well in your time and in your way.

Dandy Daughters

"Moving my father to an assisted-living facility was one of the most difficult things I've ever done," Annette shared. "I prayed about it for months and consulted friends who had gone this route before me. My three sisters and I had a family meeting and then took turns scouting facilities in our area. We wanted Dad to live within a 20-minute drive of at least one of us."

Finally Annette and her siblings chose Mountain High Assisted Living. It was a beautiful facility situated on a hill overlooking the town of San Dominic in northern Oregon. "I breathed a sigh of relief the night we moved him in, unpacked his belongings, and got Dad settled into his *new* home after more than 50 years in the house my sisters and I had grown up in."

A week later, after restless nights and a flood of tears, Annette was ready to take him out of the home and move him in with her and her husband, Hunter. "I couldn't stand thinking of Dad declining in this sterile environment surrounded by the wheelchair population." To Annette her father was still youthful and mobile. He just needed extra help.

"Imagine my surprise," she said, "when I went to visit early one morning. There was Dad, the center of attention at the breakfast table, entertaining a host of other men about the same age (80 plus). I listened in on their conversation and soon noticed they were having a ball, regaling one another with stories of their well-lived lives. When one stopped another took over."

When Annette was ready to leave that day, her father whispered in her ear, as he hugged her goodbye, "All of these men came at the urging of their daughters. Isn't that something?" He held Annette by the shoulders and looked her in the eye. "We're all so glad we found each other. Now I have a whole new group of friends."

One of the men, Annette learned, had come up with the phrase "Daughters are dandy." They made a point of repeating the words every time a daughter came to visit and when she was leaving. It became a trademark slogan for this band of cronies!

Annette blew kisses to each one as she sailed out the door. Trailing behind her was a loud chorus of old men chanting, "Daughters are dandy, daughters are dandy, dandy indeed."

Annette smiled all the way home. That night she slept like a daughter should when she knows her father is happy and well-cared for!

Reflection

O LORD, what is man that you care for him,
the son of man that you think of him? (Psalm 144:3).

Oh God, how loving you are to look after my every need from the moment I was born till the moment I pass into eternity. Thank you for guiding my every step, for helping me make wise choices, and then giving me peace of mind even in the midst of bittersweet circumstances.

Blessings Abound

Mary Ann sat across from her friend Karen as they visited over tea in Mary Ann's room at the Village Green Nursing Home. "Blessings are coming so fast I can hardly count them," Mary Ann shared.

Karen sat forward. "Tell me more." She was having a hard time believing anyone could be grateful for being in a nursing home. Maybe there was more to this "God thing" than she realized.

"First I was assigned a bed in a four-bed room in a convalescent home after the car accident. Once I got over that, I was moved to a private room in an assisted-living facility."

Mary Ann reached for Karen's hand and squeezed it. "Imagine! I was on state assistance, which provides only a semi-private room. But the owner and the marketing director gave me this perk at no extra cost!"

Karen knew Mary Ann had suffered a fracture of her fifth lumbar disc, as well as experiencing pressure on her sciatic nerve from a bulging herniated disc. That meant another month of rehab in yet another convalescent home because she couldn't walk.

"Here I am today," continued Mary Ann, "back in my private room. The director held it for me."

She raised her cup and smiled!

Karen clinked her cup against Mary Ann's. "You've inspired me," Karen said. "And you've given me a lot to think about. I've never considered being grateful for the hard times."

Mary Ann giggled. "Try it. I think you'll like it. And it's a great tonic at bedtime."

"Really?"

"As you fall asleep, count your blessings instead of sheep!"

Reflection

Who is going to harm you
if you are eager to do good? (1 Peter 3:13).

Dear Lord, you provide for me even when I'm unaware of it. Thank you for knowing what I need even before I do and then providing it in the best way.

Slippin' and Slidin'

S*now!* Everywhere Teresa looked there was snow. And there was more to come, according to the weather report. She looked around the floor in the medical center where she was a nurse and thought, *We're in for a long haul.* It was clear everyone was trapped for the rest of the day and probably through the night.

As the day wore on, Teresa began to enjoy the change in routine. The floor was much quieter than usual without the round of visitors coming and going. "Our patients were not so thankful," she admitted. "Many of them looked like pouting children. There were no relatives and friends to take their minds off their situations."

Physical therapy was cancelled since some of the therapists couldn't get to the hospital due to road conditions. The aides on hand had to improvise. The supervisor asked them to walk their patients along the corridor. Soon after, a small parade formed.

"People poured into the hallway," said Teresa, "and walked back and forth encouraging each other to keep on keeping on."

Two elderly ladies made a comical attempt at wheelchair racing. "I knew our staff would need patience, fortitude, and nutrition," Teresa commented. "So I brought up some fresh fruit and assorted snacks and sodas."

The bounty cascaded across the flowered tablecloth covering the nurses' station. Like an oasis in the desert, it became a popular spot for everyone to stop. People smiled more and helped each other get through their tasks.

Leave it to the younger generation to lighten the mood! Two nursing students wanted to take advantage of this landslide of snow by sledding down the steep driveway outside the hospital. "We don't keep sleds or boots under the counter," Teresa quipped, "so it appeared to be a lost opportunity until one of the patients told the young women to use garbage bags as boots and secure them with rubber bands."

The housekeeper even got in on the fun. She cut up two cardboard boxes to use as makeshift sleds. The young nurses went outside to try out their new equipment. The staff wheeled the patients to the windows so they could watch the show.

"We all cheered as the sledders sailed down the long hill, landed in a pile of snow, and came up giggling," said Teresa. "It was a lousy situation until our imagination and creativity kicked in. Now we all remember the fun we had the night we got snowed in."

Life is good when you make it so!

Reflection

How lovely is your dwelling place,
O LORD Almighty! (Psalm 84:1).

God, I can pout and grow weary when something unpleasant occurs or I can "save the day" with a positive attitude and a kind and caring word for others. Whether caught in a snowstorm or blessed with a day of sunshine, may I turn my heart to you in praise and thanksgiving.

A Hard Fall

Ginger walked into the kitchen and reached for her daily dose of Fosomax—the pill that was to keep osteoporosis at bay now that she was over 60 and of slender build. She had the type and size body most likely to suffer a fracture during the older years. But she practiced all the sensible things the doctor advised. She did weight-bearing exercises such as walking and biking each day, and she ate a diet high in calcium, moderate in protein, and rich in leafy green vegetables. The last thing she wanted was to fall. If she broke a bone, that could mean months of inactivity, maybe even a complete change in her lifestyle. The thought made her shiver.

Ginger walked out to the rose garden and sat down to sip her morning tea. She thought back to all the pratfalls and spills she had taken during her growing up years—one after another, yet she hadn't broken a bone yet and she wasn't about to now.

One time she fell while playing neighborhood baseball in the street across from her family's house.

"Lord, remember, how I tried to catch a ball, stumbled on our driveway, managed to get to the lawn as I fell, and hydroplaned

111

right into the sprinkler?" Ginger broke out laughing just thinking about the experience and how embarrassing it was at the time.

Another memory came to mind. This fall was still a mystery even after all these years. "I fell in the kitchen carrying a pan of gravy, somehow spilled it, sat in it, and slid across the room. How ever did *that* happen, God? Apparently you were watching, or I'd have ended up in the emergency ward."

Ginger recalled the most embarrassing moment of all, when she slipped on a wet spot in the dirt track leading up to a small stage where Gene Autry was signing autographs for all the people who came to see him sing and do rope tricks. Her feet went up the air and her skirt tumbled back over her head. How embarrassing!

"But my biggest fall was at age 17 when I fell in love with you, Lord Jesus. And I never want to recover from that!"

Reflection

The LORD upholds all those
who fall and lifts up all
who are bowed down (Psalm 145:14).

Lord, I can handle a pratfall or two. They're often good for a laugh. But I can't handle falling into sin. Help me today, dear Jesus, to cling to you, to hear your voice, to obey and follow through so that I will walk with confidence all the days of my life.

Ex-cu-use Me!

Grateful Grandma

On her birthday Sherri was bummed instead of excited, despite the lovely dinner her husband and daughter had prepared and the cake they had decorated with fresh flowers and 50 candles. She was now an official member of the "over the hill" gang, as her friend Kate, a year older than Sherri, was quick to remind her.

That evening before bed the phone rang. She was sure it would be her son Aaron calling to wish her a happy birthday and maybe even commiserate over this milestone. He was the oldest of her five children. Aaron made her laugh so she always looked forward to hearing from him.

"Hi, Mom," the masculine voice said when Sherri picked up the phone. "This is Aaron. I have some terrific news. Are you ready?"

"Sure!" Sherri hoped he'd say that he and his wife, Carolyn, were coming home for Thanksgiving.

He did have something to say regarding the month of November, but it didn't have anything to do with the national holiday.

"Mom, you're going to be a grandma. What do you think of that?"

"*Grandma?*" she blurted out. *Me? But that's what you call my mother,* she thought as her heart went thud.

"'That's terrific news," she managed to say. "How's Carolyn feeling?"

"Just fine, Mom. Really great. We hope you and Dad will come to the East Coast for the birth. The due date is right before Thanksgiving. What better way to celebrate?"

Thanksgiving at my son's house? How could this be? It seemed just yesterday that I was fixing turkey and all the trimmings for my family. Now Don and I would be guests at our son's house. Sherri could hardly take it in. Turning 50 was bad enough, but being old enough to be a grandmother seemed worse.

She congratulated her son and then her daughter-in-law and hung up. Sherri sat down and thought about what was ahead. Many of her friends had become grandmothers already, and she knew how nutty they were about their grandchildren. Maybe that could happen to her too. And then it hit her. "This first grandchild is an *extension* of the love Don and I share!" she said aloud.

Sherri jumped up and ran to the phone to call her son back and tell him how really thrilled she was. She then sat back down and wrote a love letter to the grandchild she would meet in November...at his or her house!

Reflection

I have been reminded of your sincere faith,
which first lived in your grandmother Lois and
in your mother Eunice and, I am persuaded,
now lives in you also (2 Timothy 1:5).

God, what a blessing it is to live long enough to see my children's children. They are jewels in my crown. May I never take for granted the gift of life that you have made possible by the love my husband and I share.

Senior Sipper

Marco sailed down the highway whistling to the tune on the radio. He was feeling *great!* He had just nailed a sweet deal. His sidekick, Dennis, was in awe. Marco enjoyed showing the younger man how to make things work for the client, yet take care of himself too. He dropped off Dennis at the car park. "See you tomorrow at the office," Marco shouted as he drove off.

He pulled onto the highway and congratulated himself all over again. "Not bad for a 60-plus guy breaking into a tough business. I've still got some good years ahead. By the time I retire I'll be sitting pretty. Hot dog!"

Suddenly Marco spotted a billboard for Billy's Best Burgers. *Next exit then turn right.* He pulled into the right lane, drove down the ramp, and turned into the parking lot. He was famished and thirsty and could hardly wait to dig into a hunk of meat and down a glass of iced tea. Some fries and a slice of pie, as well, would do him just fine. He had missed lunch due to the real estate caravan and then the time spent with the client.

He approached the counter, a $10 bill in hand. The young clerk took his order. "Would you like the Senior Sipper, sir? Two extra ounces over the regular size for half the price. It's Billy's way of taking care of our seniors."

Marco was shocked. *Senior? What makes him think I'm one of* those? *I'm a man about town. I have places to go and things to do.*

The clerk apparently noticed the look of surprise on Marco's face. He backpedaled fast. "Sir, I'm sorry if I...uh, may I take your order?"

Marco pressed in on the clerk. He felt his pulse elevating. "How old does one have to be to qualify for the Senior Sipper?"

"I'm not sure. I think it's 62," he mumbled.

"Well I'm 61½," Marco countered. "I'll take the regular-sized drink."

Reflection

They will still bear fruit in old age,
they will stay fresh and green (Psalm 92:14).

Dear Lord, it's hard to admit I'm aging and to know there are fewer years ahead than behind. But then I think of your promise that you have prepared a place for me in heaven and I relax. I will spend eternity with you. My life on earth is but a blip on the screen of time.

A la Mode

Patsy and Jill walked into the gym, their bright red-and-white gear bags slung over their shoulders. Both were in their early 70s now, but they remembered the good old days, some three decades ago, when they were two of the most popular aerobics instructors in town. So much for tight thighs, smooth calves, beautiful biceps, and slim waists. Now they were both doing their best to uphold one another in an attempt to recapture that fit feeling they had after a good workout. At least they hadn't gained any weight. That was encouraging.

Patsy pumped iron while Jill did push-ups. Then they each grabbed a magazine and mounted the treadmill, running and reading till they were limp. Afterward they took a hot shower, dressed for lunch, and walked toward the front door.

Eric, the manager, stepped forward and handed each one a flyer. "Beach Cities Hospital is holding a blood drive. We're helping to get the word out," he said and pointed to the contact info at the bottom of the page.

Patsy and Jill each took a flyer, thanked Eric, and walked to their cars.

"What do you say we drive over there now?" suggested Patsy.

"We can find out more, and if it's convenient, let's donate a pint and then go to lunch."

Jill nodded in agreement. "Good idea. I'm game."

The women drove off to the hospital.

Half an hour later they were standing at the Information desk at Beach Cities Hospital, reading the guidelines for donating blood. Everything checked out until they got to the topic of weight. Patsy weighed 108 and Jill weighed 102—both too slight to donate blood—"for your own safety" stated the information sheet. The minimum weight requirement was 110 pounds.

"Well, I'll be," said Patsy, planting her hands on her hips.

"The heck with this," said Jill. "Here we are working our behinds off trying to get in shape, and they won't take our good blood."

Patsy started laughing. She poked Jill. "I've got an idea. Let's cry in our coffee over a slice of apple pie with a double dip of vanilla ice cream."

Jill gave her friend a high-five as they jogged out of the hospital and headed for Hillside Pie Shop.

Reflection

For the LORD gives wisdom, and from his mouth come
knowledge and understanding (Proverbs 2:6).

Dear God, help me to be wise and discerning in all my affairs and not to take rejection personally. Standards and rules are often in my best interest, and I need to rest in that.

Surprise!

Time to Tell

Gil pulled into the driveway, lumbered out of the car, and pushed his way into the house. He was hot, sweaty, and beat! He had worked all day at the glass plant and couldn't wait to pour an iced tea and put his feet up. He noticed a message pinned to the cork board in the kitchen.

> *Gil dear, I'm at the store picking up a few things for dinner. Home by 6:00.*
>
> *Love, Patsy*

Gil glanced at his new watch, a birthday gift from his wife, to see how much time he had before her return. "Darn. The crystal's fogged over—I'm perspiring too much, I guess."

With that, Gil put the watch in the oven on warm, scribbled a reminder note to Patsy. "My watch drying in oven. Please remove." He picked up his drink and headed for the shower and a nap before dinner.

At 5:45 Patsy walked in, saw Gil snoozing in the recliner in the den, and tiptoed around the kitchen so she wouldn't wake him. *He works so hard. I'll let him rest a bit longer,* she decided.

She put a couple of frozen meals in the oven with one hand, and punched in 400 degrees with the other. She was tired too. They would kick back tonight and watch a movie while they ate.

After some time Patsy noticed a peculiar odor. She sniffed near the trash can, and then around the sink but couldn't place it. Then she noticed smoke streaming out of the oven. She yanked open the door. *Gil's brand-new watch!* The crystal was a ball of melting plastic.

She fished it out with a pair of tongs. *What in the world is this doing here?* Then she noticed a note on the sideboard in Gil's scrawl.

Oh how terrible! Why didn't I see this sooner?

Patsy listened at the door of the den. Gil's soft snore assured her he was out cold. If she hurried, she could make it to the jeweler's and back before he woke up.

She rushed into the shop and slid the watch across the counter. "Bill, look what happened to Gil's watch. Can you put on a new crystal and check for damage?"

"Sure thing. Take it easy."

Patsy paced the floor, her heart pounding and her mind racing. *God, why didn't you stop me? You could have directed me to the note.*

Her hand flew to her mouth in shame. *Oh Lord, forgive me for trying to pin this on you. I'm acting like a child.*

"Here you go..." Bill interrupted as he handed her the watch with its new crystal in place.

Patsy told Bill what had happened, and the two had a good laugh. Then she hurried home, put the watch on top of Gil's note, and proceeded to fix dinner.

Gil walked into the kitchen moments later. He stretched, kissed Patsy on the cheek, then stepped back and wrinkled his nose. "What's that smell?" he asked. "I hope it's not our dinner!"

Patsy looked at the floor. "No, not our dinner. I guess the oven needs a good cleaning, that's all. I'll take care of it after we eat."

"All right," he said. Gil reached for his watch. "Drying it in the oven was just the ticket. Good thing I left you a reminder."

"Good thing," Patsy muttered.

As she pulled a pitcher of lemonade from the fridge, she glanced at the scripture magnet on the door. "There is a time for everything, and a season for every activity under heaven" (Ecclesiastes 3:1).

Patsy put a hand to her chest and breathed. *Speaking of reminders, Lord, thanks for this one.* Then she added a verse of her own! "There is also a time to confess your mistakes to your husband."

And Patsy did just that—*after* dinner! They both had a good laugh and a long hug.

Reflection

Therefore confess your sins
to each other and pray for each other
so that you may be healed (James 5:16).

Lord, thanks for bearing with me when I try to cover my tracks, blame you, or hide from the truth. And thank you for standing with me when I confess what I've done. I feel so much better when I'm right with you and with my loved ones. Then I can laugh and really mean it!

In Darkness and in Light

Norm and Angie dated for three years before they were married. That is, if you call dating getting together for coffee or a movie or a walk when they could spare a couple of hours. Between them they had six kids—ages 14 to 20! There was always something going on with his brood or hers—soccer games, piano lessons, Girl Scouts, Little League, and so on. Sometimes the only chance Norm and Angie had to visit was over the phone while Angie stirred spaghetti sauce with one hand and held the phone with the other. Norm often called from his car while he drove to a client's office. Angie called him on her break at work.

Finally she'd had enough of this part-time romance. Angie's 14-year-old must have read her mind.

"When are we getting married?" Julia asked as Angie drove her to school one April morning.

"*We?*" Angie probed. "Aren't you and whomever you have in mind a little young to be thinking about matrimony?"

"Not *me*, Mom!" she spouted. "I mean you and Norm and all us kids?"

"Oh, *that* we! Do you think it's a good idea?"

"Yes...and so do Jamie and Lonnie and Patricia and Sam and Lily."

"It sounds as if you've taken a vote. Do Norm and I have anything to say about this?"

"You could say *yes!*"

Angie and Julia laughed, hugged goodbye, and blew each other a kiss. "See you at three, honey," Angie called.

"See ya, Mom."

Angie drove off, mulling what her daughter had said. Moments later she pulled over to the side of the road and reached for her cell phone. *Julia's right. It's time to make this happen.* Angie decided then and there to call Norm before she lost her courage.

"Hi, sweets. It's Angie. I have a proposal for you."

"Let's have it." Norm sounded rushed. *Maybe he has a client in the car. I should have asked.*

"Will you marry me?" she squeaked.

Norm gulped. "You serious?"

"Dead serious. We're both over 50. Time's running out. We need to be together. What do you say? Our kids are all for it. Julia told me."

"I say *yes!* I thought you'd never ask!" he responded.

"*I'd* never ask?" Then Angie gulped. "Great. When?"

"How about the last week in June, right after Lily graduates?"

"Sounds perfect! Gotta run. I have a wedding to plan."

Over the next month Angie felt like a monkey in a tree. She swung between a formal wedding at her church to a family thing at home. Finally they settled on a small evening ceremony at a chapel in Fairfield, a little town about 30 minutes from home. An evening wedding sounded romantic.

Friends and family pitched in to arrange flowers, food, and invitations.

The day of the wedding, Angie woke up scared. All preparations were finished. Suddenly she was filled with questions and doubts. *Am I ready? Is this what I really want?*

Heck of a time to recoil! her mind shot back.

God, help me, please. Was this your idea or mine? I can't remember. Getting married is a big step. Taking on three more kids, sharing a bathroom with someone after all these years. Norm said he snores, and he doesn't eat lasagna. That's my favorite dish. I think we're incompatible, don't you?

Of course I love him, but is that enough, Lord? Just a week ago I was so happy. Will you promise to pick me up if I keel over?

At five thirty, Julia, Patricia, Sam, and Angie piled into the car and drove to the chapel. Norm, Jamie, Lily, and Lonnie were waiting when they arrived. Friends began gathering in the pews inside, and the flowers on the altar shimmered in the light.

Angie shook inside as Pastor Frank stood before her and Norm.

"Angie, Norm, friends, and family, this evening we're gathered together..." he began. The lights suddenly went out. O-U-T as in blackout.

Gathered together in a jet-black room. Oh great! Not so much as a street lamp. And the moon? Hiding behind a tree. God, please, let there be light. You've done it before.

Julia squeezed my hand. "Mom, what are we going to do now? Come back tomorrow?"

"I hope not, honey."

Pastor Frank groped his way off the platform and returned with two lit candles.

"Shall we keep going?"

Norm nodded yes and then looked at Angie.

She nodded and grabbed his hand. *This is not the romantic wedding I had in mind.* She glanced up at Norm and her heart swelled. *But maybe it's even more romantic this way.* He looked so handsome in the candlelight. His eyes shone and his hand felt good in hers. Angie breathed and steadied herself. *God, I do love this man. Help me to be the wife he deserves. I can't do it without you.*

Norm and Angie exchanged vows. They slipped gold bands onto each other's ring finger, and Pastor Frank pronounced them man and wife. Then the children and Norm and Angie promised out loud to uphold one another in their new family. They committed to love each other in sickness and in health, in riches and in poverty. And, as Angie looked around, in darkness and in light!

Reflection

You, O LORD, keep my lamp burning;
my God turns my darkness into light (Psalm 18:28).

Lord, thank you that your grace and your watchful eyes are enough to keep me safe in all my decisions and actions.

Something's Fishy

Will stood at the kitchen counter and drummed his fingers. "Let's go! What's the hold-up?"

"Ready in a minute!" Renee shouted from the hall. "I can't find my fishing pole."

"It's in the car with the tackle box," Will called. "You put it there yourself last night. Don't you remember? You're not having a senior moment, are you?"

"If I'd remembered, I wouldn't be looking for it," Renee shot back, annoyed with herself and with her husband.

"For Pete's sake. By the time we arrive the fish will have gone to bed."

"Very funny, Mr. Seinfeld!"

They finally made it out to the car and took off. They drove in silence till they reached the turn-off for Lake Dorothy, a spot they'd heard was great for trout.

Renee sat forward and waved her right hand. "Turn left here. There. No, I mean here."

Will braked and the two jolted forward. "A little warning, please, especially in this weather. Looks like a storm is on the way."

"*You* missed the turn. Don't blame *me*."

"Yes, *I* missed it." Will grabbed the map out of Renee's hand and traced the route himself.

Renee slumped, feeling stupid. *All our preparations and for what, Lord? It's miserable outside, and it's miserable in this car with you-know-who.*

Will parked. Renee grabbed her rain jacket and fishing gear, jumped out of the car, and strode briskly to the pier.

Renee heard Will's heavy footsteps coming up behind her. *I'll find my own fishing spot, thank you very much!* she thought.

"Careful," Will called. "The planks'll be pretty slippery from the rain. Renee, are you listening?"

Renee marched forward, head held high. Then suddenly she slipped! Tush down, feet up. Jacket askew. She burst into tears.

Lord, I can't keep track of my pole. Can't read a map. Can't walk without slipping. And I can't hold my own with Will.

She sat up, and there was her husband beside her, helping her to her feet, hugging her tight, brushing her hair back with his gentle hands. "Honey, are you hurt? When I saw you slip, I thought you were going right off the pier. My heart nearly drowned."

He straightened her jacket and kissed her head and linked his arm in hers. "Didn't you hear me warn you?"

Will's words tumbled in Renee's mind. *"Didn't you hear me warn you?" Yes, I heard them, but I was too proud to heed them.*

Renee turned and wrapped her arms around her husband. She held on so tight he nearly lost his balance. Then Renee stepped back and looked up at him. She saw relief in his blue eyes and felt his warm breath shield her face from the cold.

"Thanks for loving me," she said.

"Was there any doubt?"

"Maybe for a second or two." She smiled, picked up her pole, and reached for the bait. "Right now it's time to catch some fish."

"You've 'caught' me," Will joked.

"And *you've* hooked *me*," Renee responded. "Completely."

Reflection

Pride only breeds quarrels,
but wisdom is found in those
who take advice (Proverbs 13:10).

Pride! It gets me every time. Dear God, help me to hear you sooner rather than later. Spare my loved ones the sting of my hurtful words and cruel thoughts. Let me salvage the good and toss the bad.

Empty Nest

Madeline patted Roland's paunch before clearing the table of breakfast dishes. "Time to take that off," she said. "Remember how handsome and slim you were when we married?"

Roland stacked the dishwasher and grumbled something he'd heard from his doctor, something about how difficult it is for an older man to trim his belly.

"Donuts twice a week do not help," Madeline barked, and then she regretted her harsh tone. "Honey, I'm just being supportive. I love you and want you to live to a ripe old age, that's all. Don't you want us to go into the golden years together?"

Roland grunted and walked out of the room. Madeline finished in the kitchen, and then she walked into the den to read the morning newspaper. The phone rang. She picked up the receiver but before she could say hello, she heard Roland speaking to his friend Lee on the extension.

"The bird has left the nest," said Lee.

Madeline recognized the code phrase for "My wife's out. I'm free to go."

"How about your bird?" Lee continued.

"Not yet, but any minute now," said Roland. "She has a hair

appointment at ten. I'll meet you at the donut shop at ten twenty. Gotta be home, though, by eleven thirty sharp."

Madeline waited for Roland to hang up the phone in the bedroom, then she hung up the one in the den. She had neglected to tell Roland that she had postponed her hair appointment till the next day.

"Going out for a walk," Madeline called to Roland. "I'll be back in twenty minutes, and then I have an appointment." It wasn't a lie. She did have an appointment, just not for her hair!

"Okay, I remember," shouted Roland.

Madeline jogged out the side door and slipped into the garage. She pulled out her cell phone and called Lee's wife, Rose.

"*This* bird has left the nest," she said, giggling. "Are you ready?"

"I'm flapping my wings," Rose quipped, stifling a laugh. "They're going to faint when they see us. Meet you at the donut shop in ten minutes, the booth in the back, right side, where the guys can't see us."

At ten twenty on the nose, Roland and Lee walked in, talking and laughing. Their wives waited until the men were settled with their coffee and chocolate-frosted donuts. Then the "birds" slid out of their booth, coffee cups in hand, and sauntered up to their husbands.

"Fancy meeting you here," Madeline cooed.

"Imagine bumping into the two of you," echoed Rose. "Just having a little fun while the birds are out of the nest, eh?"

Roland nearly choked on the hot coffee, and Lee's mouth flew open, chocolate frosting dribbling down his chin.

"Wanna buy a girl a refill?" Madeline asked, as she sidled up to her husband.

"And what about me, big boy?" Rose said, batting her lashes, as she slid into the booth next to her husband, and plunked down her cup.

The four burst out laughing. They clinked coffee cups and ordered another round of donuts!

Reflection

Kings take pleasure in honest lips;
they value a man who speaks the truth
(Proverbs 16:13).

Sometimes I lie, thinking I'm being playful and cunning, but more often I lie to cover my tracks, to keep from being discovered. Why am I so afraid of the truth? Even in the little things, I want to be a truth-teller so I can hold up my head and open my heart without fear of rebuke and judgment.

Treasure Hunt

Four-year-old J.R. lifted the top of the cedar chest in his grandmother Laura's bedroom. He poked through some old dresses, a felt hat, and a couple of baby blankets.

"Are some of Mommy's clothes in here from when she was a little girl?" he asked.

Laura ruffled J.R.'s head and took his hand. "Not in there. But I did save some. They're in an old dresser in the garage. Let's take a look."

J.R. ran ahead, eager for a treasure hunt. A few moments later the two were sitting on rickety chairs looking through toys and dresses and bonnets that once belonged to J.R.'s mother.

Then J.R. noticed an item that intrigued him—an 8" x 10" frame holding a collage of photos of J.R.'s Uncle Pat from when he was a little boy. In the center was a large picture of Pat bordered by wallet-sized updates from his elementary school days.

Laura noticed J.R. counting the photos by number: 1, 2, 3. He paused at a blank space and frowned. Laura pointed to the picture in the center. "This one is of Uncle Pat as a baby, and all the others were taken when he got into school. First grade, second grade, third grade," she said, as she touched each of the smaller photos. She stopped at the empty slot where the fourth grade picture should have been. "Oh I forgot about this. There's no picture of Pat in fourth grade."

J.R. turned to his grandmother with wide eyes. "Does that mean Uncle Pat was never *four?*"

Grandma Laura chuckled, and then reassured J.R. that indeed Uncle Pat had been four years old at one time. He just didn't have a picture to represent his time in *fourth* grade. Somehow it had gotten lost and never replaced.

J.R.'s forehead relaxed as he continued looking at and counting the remaining photos.

Reflection

Wisdom brightens a man's face and changes
its hard appearance (Ecclesiastes 8:1).

Dear Lord, kids do say the darnedest things! And I'm so glad they do. Their cute comments and unique questions keep me on my toes, just where I want to be as I grow older.

Young at Heart

Fifty-Five Plus

Vicky walked up to the counter at the YMCA. She picked up a brochure listing the latest classes: swimming, Pilates, yoga, stair-step, you name it. They all looked inviting. Then she spotted a special classification for the "older" crowd—referred to politely as Fifty-Five Plus! She turned the page quickly, unwilling to even check out the options. "Why wish my life away?" she murmured to herself. "There's still plenty of time. An entire year before I hit the big 55! I'm not about to take the slow lane till I get there."

She worked out, showered, changed clothes, and strolled into the noonday sun. She felt invigorated and refreshed and pleased about what she had accomplished. That afternoon she walked into the local dry cleaners to pick up a blouse and slacks. She wrote a check, and the clerk asked for her driver's license, as usual.

The woman compared the information on the two documents and then looked up at Vicky with a broad smile. "Ma'am, I see by your birth date that you qualify for our senior discount. We take one dollar off each bundle of laundry or dry cleaning. Here's a card to remind you."

Vicky forced the words from her throat. "Thank you for noticing," she said. "It's always good to save a few dollars."

"Sure is. Adds up, doesn't it?" the clerk responded.

Vicky picked up her dry cleaning, walked to her car, and got in. She put her head down on the steering wheel. "What am I thinking of? I *am* one of the 'olders' and I better get used to it. I'm 55 *this* year, not next! Well, it's back to the Y. I qualify for those 'old' classes after all. And if I can save a little money, well okay, I surrender!"

Reflection

Trust in the LORD and do good;
dwell in the land and enjoy safe pasture
(Psalm 37:3).

———————

Lord, it's not easy to watch myself growing older. I notice I want to cling to my current age. I feel much younger inside, and yet I know the birthdays are coming and going as fast as the commuter train. Keep me focused on you, dear God, and my eternal life, where I will live forever with you in paradise.

Rocking the Boat

DON'T FRET ABOUT AGING! IT'S AN OPPORTUNITY MANY DO NOT HAVE." Sally read the billboard ahead of her as she swung into the driveway of the Beach Cities Senior Center. She smiled in agreement. At age 68 she *felt* younger than she had in years. Sure, a few wrinkles creased her brow and her hands were dotted with a sprinkling of age spots, but hey, she had good health and people commented on her youthful figure. She competed in a seniors' marathon each year, and she belonged to an investment club that met each week.

But what really sustained her was her relationship with Jesus Christ. She wanted to tell the world about the positive side of aging—the gifts that are rarely mentioned or advertised on television. Gifts such as a generous spirit, an ability to love without holding back, wisdom, courage, hope, trust, gratitude, and forgiveness. Perhaps the best gift of aging is becoming a mentor for others.

And that's why she had arrived at the senior center that morning—to teach the weekly poetry class she had started the previous month. She was amazed at the talent she was uncovering as men and women poured out their thoughts and experiences on paper. Just being with them had lightened her life and given her a new purpose now that she had retired from her more than 30 years as a high school English teacher.

"Nothing's impossible with God," she mumbled to herself as she walked down the hall to her classroom. *I can do all things through Christ who strengthens me,* she prayed silently, remembering how Jesus calmed the sea when the boat he shared with his disciples threatened to send them overboard. He said, "Take courage! It is I. Don't be afraid" (Mark 6:50).

A smile crossed Sally's lips as a picture of Jesus in the boat formed in her mind. *He certainly rocked their boat,* she mused, *even as he calmed the sea. He knew what the disciples needed, and he knows what I need too.*

Sally opened the door to her classroom and strode to her desk. Her senior students looked up eagerly, pens in hand, notebooks turned to fresh pages, laptop computers humming, smiles warming the room.

"Today we're going to write about *aging,*" Sally stated, "something we know about quite well. In fact, you might say we are *experts* on the subject. Write a verse or two about the most important gift you've received as a result of reaching this stage of your life. When you're finished we'll break into groups and share those gifts with one another."

Reflection

He stilled the storm to a whisper;
the waves of the sea were hushed (Psalm 107:29).

God, thank you for rocking my boat when I most need it and for leading me across troubled waters when I am afraid.

Reunion Union

George, I'm so nervous. What if everyone looks better than we do? I mean 50 years! That's an eternity."

"Relax, Emma. You look as fabulous now as you did the day we graduated."

"You really think so?" Emma sidled up to her handsome husband as they entered the hotel and moved toward the Starlight Banquet Room where other graduates from Hillside High were filing in. "Gosh, George, thanks. I feel better already."

"Good. Let's just have fun, drop the comparison game, and keep a low profile. We have a lot to be proud of—good health, a long marriage, great kids and grandkids..."

Emma stepped back and looked at George full-face. She couldn't believe he was so calm and self-assured. He hadn't been interested in attending their fiftieth high school reunion when she'd told him about it. He said he'd moved on and didn't want to hang out with a bunch of old-timers who would probably bore the socks off him.

Emma persisted because she really wanted to go. Hillside had been such a small school when they attended; they knew everyone from freshmen to seniors. She was dying to see their former chums, to talk, and to reminisce.

"All right," he had agreed, "under one condition."

"And that is?"

"That you behave yourself and don't go on and on about our lives. Some people might not be as fortunate as we are, and I don't want to add to their pain."

Emma looked at George as though he'd gone over the edge. "*Me? Talk too much? Me? Behave inappropriately?*" *Ever since I've known this man,* Emma mused silently, *he's been the class clown, the president of this and that, the "mayor" of Breckendridge Drive, where we live, and the one who puts his foot in his mouth more often than in his shoe!*

She tapped him on the side of his head with her purse and rolled her eyes. "Okay," she said, "I'll behave if you do. But if you let loose, expect anything."

Now here they were among their old friends. They pushed through the crowd and located their table. Bebe and Roy Parsons were already seated. Emma was thrilled to see them. Bebe had been a year behind Roy, Emma, and George, but they were all good friends. Bebe and Roy married the same day as Emma and George, and then moved across the country. The couples exchanged Christmas cards but hadn't actually seen one another, except in photos, in 50 years. What a blessing it was to Emma to sit down with them and others and begin sharing what had happened over the past five decades.

After dinner, the emcee invited various individuals to come to the stage and share, in a sentence or two, something they had accomplished that was especially meaningful to them.

After about 30 minutes of this, George turned to Emma and whispered, "It's happened. I'm *bored* out of my socks. If I have to listen to any more of this phony baloney I'm going to pass out."

Just then, the emcee invited George and Emma to the front—together. He went on and on about how amazing they were, the only couple who graduated and married within the same class, and even more terrific, had remained together for nearly half a century. After a round of embarrassing applause, he asked them to say a few words.

Emma didn't dare open her mouth after the warning George had issued. "The mic is all yours, Mr. Smarty-Pants," she chided softly as she stepped back and he stepped forward.

"I haven't done a darn thing since I left school," George said with a poker face. " I married a rich young woman," he added, "and never had to work!"

I should have known his wicked sense of humor would take over, Emma thought.

Hushed comments and bits of laughter rolled across the room.

George, I'll get you for this, Emma vowed silently. The emcee then turned to Emma and asked if she had anything to add. By golly, she did! Emma took the mic from his hand, turned to her husband, and without a second thought asked, "And what is your *rich* wife's name?"

With that George pulled his foot out of his mouth, returned to the table, and dug into his "just dessert"—a healthy slice of humble pie!

Reflection

When pride comes, then comes disgrace,
but with humility comes wisdom (Proverbs 11:2).

Lord, sometimes it pays to keep my mouth shut, and sometimes it pays even more to speak my mind—especially when it's called for!

Senior Discount

Lou and Wendy were driving home from the grocery store. Wendy piped up, "Lou, let's eat out tonight. I'm too tired to cook, and you've had a big day in the yard. It'll do us both good to let someone else serve us."

Lou mulled over the idea. He preferred eating at home. He liked Wendy's simple cooking and the peace and quiet of their own dining room with their choice of music. But he could tell from the fatigue in his wife's eyes that she was ready for a little TLC. Still, he resisted plunking out a $20 bill for even the most economical meal. In fact, he realized, *I'm resisting a lot of things these days. Gettin' older. Mowing the lawn. Ads for hearing aids. Senior discount coupons. Maybe I'm 61, but I don't need a hand yet.*

Wendy seemed to pick up on his mood. She opened her purse and pulled out a discount coupon for the Soup and Salad Wagon and waved it in front of him. "I have a little incentive right here."

"Another darned coupon?" he asked. "I hate those things. They make me feel old, like I'm dependent on someone else to take care of me."

"Lou, puleeze! It's a restaurant, not a nursing home. I love it that we get a little extra attention at our age and that people want to bless us with special prices. If you changed your attitude, you might even enjoy it."

Lou swung into the parking lot behind the restaurant. Then he and Wendy headed for the front door.

"I'm famished," said Wendy. "How about you?"

Lou nodded but kept his thoughts to himself.

After a hearty meal Lou and Wendy walked to the car in silence. Lou had to admit the buffet was more than he imagined. Great roast beef and gravy, whipped potatoes like his mother used to make, and desserts to die for—especially the double fudge cake.

"That wasn't so bad, was it?" Wendy teased, as Lou pulled out of the parking lot. "And think of the money we saved. The discount really helped."

Lou turned to his wife and grinned. "I just realized what's going on with me and senior discounts," he said. "I like getting the price break, but I hate admitting that I qualify for it!"

Reflection

Those who complain will accept instruction (Isaiah 29:24).

Lord God, please help me to accept myself as I am— not younger, not older, not smarter, not wiser, but who you made me to be. May I turn from complaining and comparing to thanking and praising.

Missing Parts

The Other Shirl

Shirl and her husband, Mel, raced around the house at the last moment. They had ordered movie tickets online for themselves and their friends Jim and his wife, referred to as "the *other* Shirl."

"I laid the receipt on the coffee table in the den," Shirl called from the bedroom, where she was touching up her lipstick and looking for her pink sweater.

"Not here," Mel called back.

"Where could it be? I put it there myself." Shirl ran into the den and there on the coffee table was the receipt.

"Here it is. How could you have missed it?" Shirl let out a long breath, tucked the paper into her purse, and headed for the front door. "Mel, we'll be late if we don't get into the car this minute. What's going on?"

"Can't find my glasses," Mel shouted from the living room. "I was sure I left them on the end table after reading the newspaper."

Shirl let out another long breath. *Well, that explains why he couldn't find the movie tickets receipt.*

"I knew you should have ordered a spare pair...too late now. Let's go. I'll fill you in on the plot if you can't see well enough."

"I'll get by," Mel muttered and off they went.

They picked up "the other Shirl" and her husband, Jim. While waiting in line at the theater, Jim started fiddling with his hearing aid. It squawked and squeaked as he tried to adjust it to the right volume. Then he realized the batteries were low. "I guess I'll have to make do without them," he told the others.

The women looked at each other and rolled their eyes. Mel's Shirl had told Jim's Shirl about Mel's misplaced glasses and now Jim's Shirl would have a "husband story" of her own. After the movie the couples stopped at Reggie's Deli for a cold drink and a sandwich. As they were about to eat, "the other Shirl" leaned in and said in a loud voice, "Okay, Mel...you tell Jim what you *heard*...and Jim, you tell Mel what you *saw!*"

The four cracked up laughing. Shirl and "the other Shirl" gave each other a high five.

Reflection

Forget the former things;
do not dwell on the past (Isaiah 43:18).

———————————

Lord, the changes I face are annoying and sometimes embarrassing, but you encourage me to keep going forward and to let go of the things of the past. Even though my hearing and my eyesight are not what they once were, it doesn't matter when it comes to my relationship with you. You have given me eyes to see and ears to hear your Word.

Telling the Tooth

Marlene heard from her mother that Uncle Henry, her favorite of three uncles, was declining. She wanted to see him while he was still able to communicate, so she made a trip to the nursing home in Ohio where he lived.

Marlene remembered Henry as a fun person to be with. When she was a kid he was right there with her brother and her ready to climb a tree, take on Marlene in a game of croquet, or play checkers again and again till *she* won!

Marlene looked forward to the visit. She brought along a photo album to share and reminisce over. Despite his frail body, Uncle Henry still had a bit of spunk. He enjoyed looking at all the photos of times past: Thanksgiving at Marlene's family's home, summers at the cottage in Wauconda, making angels in the snow in winter. He had never married, so he was especially close to Marlene's mother—his sister—and her family. He had been a part of Marlene's life since the earliest days.

Just as she turned the page to a new set of photos, he suddenly pushed himself to his feet and shuffled to the bathroom, muttering something about not having the control over his bodily functions he once had.

After a moment or two, Marlene heard the toilet flush, then a giant sneeze, and a muffled yell...or was it a cry for help? She bolted out of the chair and ran to the door. "Uncle Henry? It's Marlene. Are you all right? Do you need a nurse?"

With that, the door popped open and out stepped Uncle Henry, a toothless grin on his face. It seems his "lack of control" had reached new depths. As he flushed the toilet, he said, he sneezed, which shot his false teeth out of his mouth directly into the toilet bowl as it emptied.

"Well if that doesn't beat all," he quipped. "I can't see well enough anymore to watch television or read a book. I can't hear worth a darn, even with these blasted hearing aids. I need a walker if I go beyond this room, and now my teeth are gone so I can't eat. I think I'm checking out! What do you think?"

Marlene called the nurse and explained the situation, then assured Uncle Henry she would arrange for a new upper plate. She told him not to worry.

He and Marlene enjoyed the remaining moments of her visit, and when they said goodbye he pulled her close. "I'll be waiting for you in heaven," he said. "I'll have the croquet game set up, and I'll reserve the checkerboard. I love you, Marlene. Glad you got here before I took the next cloud to heaven!"

Reflection

The man who was dying blessed me (Job 29:13).

Lord, it's hard to say goodbye to those I love, but you have assured me that we will meet again in heaven. Thank you for preparing a place for me that is beyond anything I can imagine.

Seeing Is Believing

Virginia was diagnosed with macular degeneration. What a blow! It made a huge impact on her life. She could no longer enjoy the many things she had taken for granted for so long, such as reading and even watching movies and television. She had to get a special monitor for her computer, and she could no longer drive.

Everything she wanted to do had to be considered in a new way due to the change in her eyesight. Art and knitting and card playing were now a struggle, whereas a decade before they were a part of her regular routine.

Virginia received treatment for two years. During one of her checkups she felt hopeful for the first time in months. "I was overjoyed that I could read the big 'E' on the eye chart. During previous appointments I wasn't able to read any of the letters," she said.

Virginia couldn't help but blurt out her excitement over her progress. "Now may I have my driver's license back?"

The assistant winked. "When you get on the road," she quipped, "call and let us know, so we can get off!"

Reflection

And I—in righteousness I will see your face; when I awake, I will be satisfied with seeing your likeness (Psalm 17:15).

Dear Lord, the prospect of failing eyesight is frightening to think about and even more scary to endure. But I have your promise that you will always be with me, so I trust that even if my eyes fail me, you never will. You will guide me all the days of my life on earth and forever after.

Costly Secret

id woke up on Monday morning, walked to the park and back, ate breakfast, and enjoyed a cup of coffee with his wife, Dede, on the patio overlooking their rose garden. He excused himself to go to the bathroom. After taking care of business, he turned, glanced in the toilet bowl and panicked. He saw blood. His first thought was to rush out and tell Dede, but he didn't want to upset her. "I'll handle this myself," he said to his reflection in the mirror.

Over the next several weeks Sid made several medical appointments, first with his primary care provider and then with a gastroenterologist. He went through the discomfort of an Upper GI, Lower GI, barium enema, and finally a colonoscopy at the hospital. When he had to follow a special diet—for the tests—he told Dede he just wasn't feeling well. And each time he left the house, he told Dede he was running an errand, picking up gardening supplies, meeting a friend for coffee, or spending the day golfing. She didn't ask any questions since these were routine outings for Sid over the course of their marriage.

Meanwhile, Sid was sleeping fitfully, his heart was palpitating at just the thought of the next procedure, and he lost his appetite.

His mind had a field day. He imagined surgery at the very least and colon cancer at the worst.

On several occasions he came close to telling Dede, but then backed down. He missed sharing such a serious milestone in his life, and he longed for the comfort of her arms and her prayers. But still he couldn't bring himself to talk about it until he had more information to share. He didn't want to scare her.

A week after the final procedure he received word from his doctor that all test results were negative. He was given a clean bill of health. The lab work did not show any sign of blood. What a relief! *Maybe it was simply a hemorrhoid,* Sid thought. *Why didn't I think of that sooner?*

Sid was so elated that he went to Dede immediately. "Put on your prettiest dress," he said. "I'm taking you out for dinner tonight—maybe even dancing, if you can keep up with me!" He felt as though he could take on the world.

"What's gotten into you?" she asked, wrinkling her brow in confusion. "You hate to dance, and you're not all that excited about eating out. You don't like spending money on food we can cook at home."

"I have something important to tell you. I want to do so over a candlelight dinner."

"All right," she agreed. "I'll be ready."

That night the couple walked into Harbor Lights Restaurant and were led to a cozy booth overlooking the water.

"I can't wait another minute," said Dede. "What is it? Did you win the lottery? Book a cruise? Buy a new car? Tell me, please."

Sid smiled, reached across the table and took her hand. Then he gave her a detailed report on what had been going on secretly over the last couple of months. "So now you know," he said and squeezed her hand. "Looks like you're stuck with me for a few more years. I hope you're as happy about it as I am."

Dede returned his gaze and then threw her head back in a hearty laugh. "Oh Sid! You are precious! Remember when Nan and Paul gave us fresh beets from their garden about two months ago? Well…"

"What's that got to do with my good news?" Sid probed, feeling hurt by her laughter.

"Beet juice is about the same color as blood. It runs right through us. I can see where you'd mistake the color of the beets for blood in your stool."

Sid sank in his seat and sighed. Then he sat up and laughed. "What a chump!" he said. "All that time and money and embarrassment. A costly secret. If I had told you the first day, I could have saved myself a lot of worry and trouble."

"But if you *had* told me," said Dede, "we wouldn't be sitting here having a romantic, candlelight dinner. And dancing after dessert!"

Sid reached over and kissed Dede in front of he didn't care who. "You're the best!" he exclaimed.

Reflection

"Can anyone hide in secret places
so that I cannot see him?"
declares the LORD (Jeremiah 23:24).

Lord, you know my innermost secrets and desires, fears, and trepidations. May I look to you first when I am afraid, instead of taking matters into my own hands and then being disappointed with the results.

Lost and Found

Pen in Hand

Hildy noticed that her husband's hands shook a bit. The fork was unsteady when Bud ate, and when they held hands she felt a tremor. It made her sad, especially since Bud was still so sharp mentally. Oh well, this was just one more thing to add to the list of old age symptoms. She dropped the thought and focused on being thankful they had each other...as well as good minds.

She was also proud (and sometimes annoyed) that Bud was meticulous about putting things back in their rightful places. It saved a lot of frustration in their marriage. He was also quick to remind Hildy to do the same, since she was the more casual of the two. If that trait diminished then she'd know her husband really was slowing down.

Later that week, while Hildy sat in her recliner writing on her lapboard, Bud suddenly got up from his chair and walked over to hers.

"He took my pen right out of my hand," she said, "while I was in the middle of a sentence! He laid down a piece of paper on my lapboard, signed his name, and then returned my pen— all without saying a word. I was perplexed. Why use *my* pen, I wondered. He has a lovely pen of his own, and he always knows exactly where it is. In fact, I'm usually the one borrowing *his* pen."

Hildy studied Bud for a moment, waiting for him to say something. "Just then he turned around and held up his left hand. It was holding a pen—his favorite one."

He wrinkled his brow, chuckled aloud, then shook his head from side to side in a curious way. "I suppose you're wondering what I'm up to."

Hildy stifled a smile. "The thought had crossed my mind."

"Well then, I'll tell you," Bud teased. "I got up, picked up my pen to sign this form, and then for the life of me I couldn't find it." He scratched the bald spot on his head. "I hunted around the cushions on the couch, on top and under the end table, and even looked on the floor, but it wasn't anywhere that I could see. So I decided to borrow yours."

Then he looked again at the pen in his hand. "Well, at least I didn't *lose* my pen!" he said as he walked back to his chair and took up his evening newspaper.

Reflection

Cast all your anxiety on him
because he cares for you (1 Peter 5:7).

———————————

Lord, I feel anxious when I think I'm losing it, but then I remember that you have counseled me not to worry. I am to come to you with the faith of a child. Sure enough, whenever I do you show me your strength is sufficient in all situations.

Flowers for Nanny

Marjorie packed her bag, loaded it into her car, and moved from one dear person to the next, hugging and kissing each one and saying goodbye.

She turned to her daughter Debra. "It's been a great Easter weekend, honey. Thanks for everything. We'll be in touch soon. Next time I hope you'll all come to *my* corner of the world."

"Drive safe, Mom, and stop when you feel tired, okay? No shame in getting off the road for a rest," said Debra's husband, David. "We love you and want you safe."

God, thank you for this darling family, Marjorie prayed silently as tears slid down her face.

Tony and Lulu squeezed her tight. "Nanny, I love you," said Tony.

"Me too," echoed Lulu.

"Come back, okay?" begged three-year-old Rex.

"Okay," she said. "It's a deal."

Marjorie hopped into her car and backed it down the driveway. She waved. Suddenly Debra waved her arms back and forth.

"Mom, wait! Oh I'm sorry. I just realized we forgot to give

you the flowers we bought for you. The kids'll want to be in on this too. Hold on, okay?"

"Sure, honey. I'm in no rush." She got out of her car.

Debra called the three children. No response. "Where'd they go? They were right here just a minute ago," she commented.

Debra's brother-in-law, Dick, said he saw them run around the side of the house. "Hey kids," he called in the direction of the backyard, "it's time to give Nanny her flowers before she goes home."

The next moment Tony, Lulu, and Rex stood in a row, each one proudly holding a freshly picked tulip—the ones that had been growing profusely along the side of the garage. No one had told them that "Nanny's flowers" were in a store-bought basket hanging just out of sight in the breezeway.

Holding the basket, Debra ran up to her mother just as Marjorie took the lovely tulips from each grandchild. Tears filled her eyes again. She walked to the car, her arms filled with flowers and her heart filled with love.

Reflection

Flowers appear on the earth;
the season of singing has come,
the cooing of doves is heard
in our land (Song of Solomon 2:12).

How lovely, O Lord, are the flowers of the field and the grass of the land. Thank you for these amazing gifts of color and beauty and gentleness. May I find your hand in each blossom and blade.

Time's Up

Chaz and his wife, Arlette, prepared for a crew to come in and begin updating their kitchen. That meant emptying shelves, cabinets, cubbyholes, and the pantry—no small chore after living in their house for 35 years.

A week before the start date, Arlette was called out of town on business. This left the dirty work to Chaz.

"Before you leave," he said, "I'd like us to agree on something so I don't have to phone you about whether to keep or toss every little item."

"Fine. How do you want to work it?"

"Let's agree that if we haven't used an item in two years or more, I pitch it or give it to a charity."

Arlette looked up, touched her chin in thought, opened and closed drawers and cabinets, then gave Chaz a nod of approval. "You're on," she said. "I don't think there will be much to debate, but I'm happy to go along with your plan."

She left the next morning. Chaz rolled up his shirt sleeves that day and started sorting and assessing everything from an old pot without a lid to a pair of rusty tongs. He made three piles: Keep, Toss, Give Away.

By noon he was feeling great. He had reduced the clutter to the point that everything left fit nicely on the dining room table and on the floor beneath it.

The workers arrived two days later, and the demolition process began.

The following week, Arlette came home and was delighted to find that Chaz had not gone overboard, as she suspected he might. He was the tosser in the family, and she was the keeper.

Eight weeks later the kitchen was ready for use. Chaz and Arlette awakened the next day ready to return every item to its new and rightful place. But as Arlette went through the baking pans, cooking pots, and mixing bowls, some of her favorite cooking tools were missing.

"Chaz, where did you put...? What did you do with...? I can't find..."

"Sorry, hon," he said with a grin. "Time was up on all that stuff. Haven't used them in two years or more, remember?"

"This is horrible," she said, "I never should have agreed to such a deal. Wouldn't you know it? *Tonight* is the very night I planned to make a pot roast in our Dutch oven, bake muffins in our cupcake tin, and whip potatoes with the old hand blender!"

"Sure!" he teased. "You haven't made a meal like that in the last five years."

Arlette folded her arms and lifted her head. "Well then, you'll just have to take me out to dinner—every night this week—because the menu I had planned requires nearly every item you gave away. Too bad I wasn't home to advise you of my plans!"

Chaz caught the twinkle in her eye. He wrapped his arms around Arlette and drew her close. "I'll let you get away with it this week," he said, "but starting Monday night, we'll be using all the *new* cookware I purchased while you were away." Then he pulled out a large box from the hall closet and presented it to her with a big kiss.

Reflection

A generous man will himself be blessed (Proverbs 22:9).

Dear Lord, it's fun to laugh and share and tease the people I love. I sense that you are delighted when we do loving things for one another. You are the model of generosity. Thank you for showing me how to give from my abundance, which came from you.

Forget Me Not

J anie had just about had it with her aging mother. It seemed the elderly woman was losing one thing after another, and the cost of replacing the items was adding up. First a hairbrush, then a sweater, and now her hearing aids. She knew the bean-sized gizmos cost nearly as much as a used car!

"Mom, I know it's getting more difficult to remember things, but I want you to try. When you put something down, put it *out* on a table or on the bed so I can see it. Then I'll be glad to put it where it belongs."

Her mother nodded and lowered her head. Janie felt terrible. She wasn't so young herself, and her memory wasn't the best either. Why was she landing on her poor mom who needed her support, not her criticism?

Janie put her arms around her mother, hugged her, and asked her forgiveness. They sat down to dinner and Janie did her best to make conversation, but it was no use. Her mother couldn't hear a thing without her hearing aids.

The following day Janie dropped everything she was doing when she heard a loud thud in the bathroom. She rushed through the door, and there was her mother on the floor on her backside. She had tripped on a corner of a small floor mat. Fortunately she landed on the plush bath rug instead of on the hard tile.

Janie's heart pounded as she helped her mother up and into a chair. She checked for bruises but none appeared.

"Mom, you're going to be okay," Janie reassured her, mouthing each word slowly so her mother would get what she was saying.

When she returned to her desk in the den, Janie began planning in her mind that she would enroll her mother in adult daycare where she would be supervised for several hours a day while Janie worked.

Janie walked into the bedroom and plopped down on the bed for a moment to pull herself together. Something poked her bottom. She jumped up and there was a pair of glasses—the delicate frames bent at an odd angle and one of the lenses loose.

M-o-t-h-e-r! she shouted in her mind. *Will this never end?*

Janie picked up the glasses and marched into the living room. She was about to give her mother another lecture about misplacing her possessions. As she held up the frames to make her point, she suddenly realized they were *her* specs, not her mother's. She backed out of the room quietly, holding on to her hasty remarks.

"Like mother, like daughter," she muttered and then burst out laughing. "I guess we'll both be enrolling in adult daycare if I keep this up."

Reflection

But how can I bear your problems and your burdens
and your disputes all by myself?
(Deuteronomy 1:12).

Lord, I feel overwhelmed when I face conflict and forget-fulness in myself or others. Thank you for showing me that I am never alone, that you are always with me.

Checkup or Checkout

Vicky woke up, looked in the mirror, and squealed. "Where did you come from?" she demanded of each new wrinkle. "Sneaking up on me in the middle of the night, are you? Well take that, and that, and that," she sputtered as she plastered her face with a cucumber-based cream that was meant to soften the lines around her eyes and mouth.

She was fed up with these obvious signs of aging. How unfair! She didn't *feel* like 69, but her face showed it. And it didn't help her ego one bit when her young female neighbor suggested she do something to perk herself up—such as buying new lingerie at Victoria's Secret. *Easy for her to say! She's 29, not 69. Victoria and I may share the same name, but we have very different tastes in underwear.*

A friend recently told her to stop celebrating birthdays. "Your age is just a number in your mind," she added. "Personally I'm 55 and will be till the day I die."

But Vicky came up against the last straw when she went to see the dermatologist about a worrisome sore on her back. She slipped into the paper gown, sat on the exam table, and waited— and waited and waited some more. Vicky browsed through six magazines and still no sign of the doctor.

Finally she stuck her head out the door to ask a nurse what was going on. The lights were off in the hallway, and there was no sound except the soft ticking of the clock on the wall.

"Anyone here?" she called.

Vicky padded a few steps when suddenly she was face-to-face with an older gentleman. "Are you one of the doctors?" she asked in a faint voice.

"Oh no, ma'am. I'm from the cleaning service."

That did it. Vicky scampered back to the exam room, jumped into her clothes, and ran out the door.

"Friends have told me that LOLs (little old ladies) are invisible to most of the population," she muttered, as she slid into her car, "but I didn't believe it till today! Time to change doctors—again."

Reflection

I will rescue them from all the places where they were scattered on a day of clouds and darkness (Ezekiel 34:12).

———————————

Dear Lord, some of these situations are downright funny and some are downright pathetic. I don't know whether to laugh or cry. So I'll turn to you in my disappointment, knowing you will never forget or overlook me, no matter what I do.

Brush Off!

Janice stepped into the bed and bath store and stamped her snowy boots on the floor mat. She loosened her heavy scarf from around her neck and let it hang loose over the back of her shoulders. She pulled off her gloves and cap and placed them in the cart.

Now she was ready for some serious shopping. New sheets, new pillowcases, new bath towels and for sure a new toilet brush. The one she had was no good anymore. All the bristles had gone flat.

While she strolled through the store, she found many wonderful items on sale: fancy bar soap, shower gel, guest towels, and a cute shell-shaped lotion dispenser—a luxury but one that fit her décor and was at a good price.

Janice was relieved by the time she got to the checkout counter. She had braved the cold, snowy day, and she was glad she had. Now she could cross off several items on her to-do list. She got in line, leaned over the cart, and piled her items on the conveyor belt. She picked up a magazine on the rack and leafed through it while the checker rang up her purchases and bagged them.

Janice swiped her credit card, tucked the receipt into her purse, and was on her way. She strode to the parking lot when suddenly a stranger approached her.

He held up a familiar looking item—the toilet bowl brush she had just purchased.

"I noticed this hanging off your scarf in back," he said, chuckling. "It's an attention-getter, I'll say that."

Janice was mortified. Then she realized how it might have happened. When she leaned over the cart, the loose end of her knitted scarf caught on the bristles and they stuck. She made an about-face and headed back to the store to pay for the brush. She hoped the clerk would not haul her off to jail for shoplifting!

Reflection

The one who trusts in him
will never be put to shame (Romans 9:33).

Lord, I'm red in the face and hot under the collar when someone catches me unaware, especially when I feel so together. I'm thankful that I can always hold up my head in your presence because you never make me feel ashamed.

Pets and People

A Better Man

When Russ bought his Yellow Lab, Lester, he had no idea the dog would make a man out of him. "I had planned to make him an obedient pet," said Russ. "So I took him to dog training school. He learned to sit, stay, go down, come, and hold his bark. After a time, he was the most reliable and gentle dog I ever owned."

Russ never worried about leaving the patio doors and windows wide open in his Arizona home. He knew Lester wouldn't run away or jump on visitors when they turned up at the door. Even Miss Manners would have been impressed with his behavior in nearly every situation.

Not so with Russ, however.

His wife had been telling him for months that he lost control when he got upset and he was scaring the entire family. His voice boomed as he let off steam. "That volume was fine when I sang in a local opera company," he confessed, "but not fine in my own home with our children in the next room and neighbors on both sides of our house."

One day topped all the rest. He had received a speeding ticket on his way home from the swim club. He had been only five minutes from home when an officer pulled him over. He walked in roaring about the injustice.

The kids scattered and Russ' wife, Maria, took to the garage while Russ carried on at the top of his lungs. Lester, in his inimitable way, did the only thing that made sense—and that got Russ' attention. He looked at his master as though he had lost his mind, meandered out the patio door, and headed down the road. Just like that. Russ wondered if this time the dog had had enough.

Maybe he won't come back, Russ worried. *Maybe my wife and kids won't return either.*

"I pulled myself together," Russ admitted, "calmed down with prayer, regrouped my thoughts, and reached for my checkbook to pay the fine. Then I ran down the street and begged Lester to come home. He looked at me with those big dark eyes, and trotted alongside me as we headed back.

"I called Maria and the kids into the den and hugged each one. 'Lester taught me to be a better man,' I said. 'I'm not sure how he did it, but he did. I love each one of you, and I'm sorry for scaring you. Will you forgive me?' "

The family huddled together in a group hug. Lester wormed his way into the center, ready to take credit where credit was due!

Reflection

A gentle answer turns away wrath,
but a harsh word stirs up anger (Proverbs 15:1).

There I go again, making a to-do over nothing. Lord, I need your grace and your strength to overcome my childish behavior when I feel misunderstood or mistreated, even when it's justified. Thank you for never leaving or forsaking me, no matter how out of control I get.

Doggy Doo!

"Howard, it's your turn to call about that dog. I think we'll get better results if the authorities hear a man's voice." Flo was adamant this time.

"Why do I have to be the fall guy? What if the dog belongs to one of our neighbors? I don't want any problems on this block."

"Problems on this block? What about problems in this *house?*" Flo let out a sigh and walked out of the yard and into the kitchen. *He complains too, but he won't do anything about it. He likes Plan A—status quo. I'm for Plan B—confront and move on.*

Flo heard some commotion in the front of the house. She looked out just as the German police dog was relieving himself on their lawn. That did it!

"Howard, come quick. See what I mean? Not only is this character a darn nuisance with all that barking and trampling lawns, but now he's picked our yard for his bathroom."

Flo was late for school, so she left the conversation unfinished, said goodbye, and jumped into the car. As she backed out of the drive, she saw Gloria Adams, her neighbor and boss, the principal of Shady Oaks Elementary School where Flo was a third grade teacher. Flo stopped and called out the window to Howard. "Honey, hold off on the phone call. I'm going to ask Gloria if she's been bothered by the dog, and if she knows the owner. Maybe we can get a petition going...you know the old saying, 'strength in numbers.'"

Howard nodded. "Good idea. Let me know what happens."

Ten minutes later Flo pulled into the school parking lot and hurried off to her classroom. During the morning break, she walked into the teachers' lounge, poured a cup of coffee, and sat down to enjoy a few minutes of quiet.

The principal passed by the doorway and Flo jumped up, hoping to catch her before she went into a meeting.

"Gloria, do you have a sec? I've been meaning to ask you about the German police dog I've seen running around our neighborhood. Do you by chance know the owner? I'd like to meet..."

"Why yes. Freddy belongs to my daughter. We're taking care of him while she's on vacation. You can meet her when she returns on Friday. Drop by after dinner. Great dog, eh? Are you thinking of getting one too?"

"Oh yeah, great dog," Flo muttered. "We're, well, we're not sure we're ready for a dog...but..."

"No worries. Cindy can tell you everything you need to know."

Flo pulled out her cell phone and called her husband. "Regarding the dog—Plan A in effect," she said in a hurried voice. "Will tell you more when I get home."

Reflection

Do not be quickly provoked in your spirit,
for anger resides in the lap of fools (Ecclesiastes 7:9).

God, I notice I want to take annoying matters into my own hands, regardless of whether or not I have enough information about a particular person or situation. Please help me turn to you first and then to follow the guidance you provide. Only you have all the facts and the perfect solution to even the most upsetting circumstance.

Rat!

Here, Brian. Grab a towel. It's your turn to wipe the pots and pans. And Betsy, you put away the silverware, okay? Then we can watch a movie and pop some corn with real butter and plenty of salt. How does that sound?"

Nonie's nephew and niece were staying the weekend with their aunt, and she was having a wonderful time spoiling them with treats. She did require help with chores while they visited, but never anything arduous. She also enjoyed playing games, catching them by surprise when they least expected it, and chasing them around the house with a dish towel, snapping at their arms and heels as they dodged and squealed. At the end of a good romp, the three crashed on the sofa in a fit of laughter.

Nonie usually got the upper hand—until that evening. She hung over the sink, scouring a pan, when suddenly she felt something crawling up the back of her blouse.

Brian and Betsy started to giggle. Then suddenly they were laughing hysterically. Nonie screamed. "Brian, check my back. Quick!"

His faced flooded with guilt. Nonie suddenly realized what was going on. She screamed again as she reached around and felt a furry creature about to pop over her shoulder. She grabbed the poor thing by its body and threw it on the floor. Nonie fled the house, letting the screen door bang behind her.

The rat recovered and so did Nonie. And Brian and Betsy were invited back again—after a period of cooling off. Even the pet rat was welcome. Soon Nonie and Pat the rat became friends.

Reflection
From six calamities he will rescue you (Job 5:19).

Dear Lord, what a comfort to know you will deliver me from one calamity after another, even something as minor as a scary prank! You do love me, and I love you.

Little Mother

Penny hauled the large bag of dog food out of the shopping cart, into her car, and then into the house when she arrived home one Monday morning. "Whew! I'm wiped out." She turned to Rodney, her Great Dane, and looked him in the eye. "See what I go through for you." Then she ran a hand over his strong back. "But you're worth it."

That afternoon she called her neighbor Mona to help her pour the dog food into plastic bins in the barn to keep out the mice. As the women poured, bits of paper fell into the first bin along with the nuggets of food. Penny reached down and picked out some of the paper. There she found six tiny mice in a paper nest. But the mother was nowhere to be found.

Penny looked at Mona. "What am I going to do? We can't abandon these little ones. They'd starve."

Then she remembered her other neighbor's son, Ryan, whose hamster had just given birth to a litter of eight. The little mother was still nursing her newborns. When Ryan found out about the mice his eyes brightened. "Maybe Silky would feed the mice," he said. "Let's see what she'll do."

Ryan's mom, Sue, came onboard too. Carefully she laid

one mouse in the far corner of the hamster cage and within seconds, Silky rushed over to it. At first Ryan and the women were concerned she'd kill the intruder. But on the contrary, Silky grabbed hold of it as though it were her own and placed it among her babies.

Penny imagined her thinking to herself, *What are you doing over there all alone? Come here right now.* Ultimately she accepted all 6 mice and fed 14 babies as long as they needed her.

Penny dabbed her eyes and clutched her chest. *What a sweet thing to see.* She knew God was using this powerful experience to remind her that no matter how far she roamed or how lost she might become, he would search her out, find her, and bring her home.

Reflection

The Lord will keep you from all harm—
he will watch over your life (Psalm 121:7).

Dear God, you say in the Bible that you will always watch over your people. They know you, and you know them. Thank you for making sure that when I am lost, I am found by you.

Hands Up!

Spunky Senior

Maxine and her elderly neighbor, Judith, enjoyed talking over the fence during the years they lived next door to each other. Maxine recalled the month Judith turned 89. "My family and I made a fuss about the fact that she had only one year to go before she was 'really' old!"

Judith took the teasing with good humor. Maxine admired her for continuing on as she had done most of her adult life, taking care of herself and her home, and hanging out her laundry because she liked the fresh scent of sunshine and clean air in her linens and towels. She was also a wonderful friend to many, and she enjoyed excellent health for her age.

"I'm doing all I can," Judith often said, "to stay in good shape. I don't mind living alone except for one thing. I'm afraid of having a heart attack in the middle of the night with no one around."

Maxine sympathized with her, imagining how frightening that would be. The women discussed the possibility of Judith wearing a medical alert necklace that would allow her to press a button for immediate aid. "She agreed it would be a good idea," said Maxine, "but I don't believe she did anything about it."

After that, Maxine and her husband kept an eye on Judith. "I began calling once a day to check in, to see if she needed anything from the store, or to see if Lou could lend a hand with a chore."

Everything was fine for several weeks. Maxine felt good about their connection and even though Judith never admitted it, Maxine felt certain she appreciated the daily calls.

Then one day during a routine phone conversation Maxine picked up a bit of anxiety in Judith's voice. "Is anything wrong?" she asked.

"I had a scare during the night," Judith said, her voice a bit shaky.

Suddenly Maxine felt nervous, fearing Judith had fallen and broken a bone. "What happened?"

"Someone broke in last night," Judith blurted. "I woke up to a stranger standing over my bed. I must have forgotten to lock the slider to my bedroom. His voice was really calm, but I didn't like it when he put his hands on my shoulders and asked for all my money."

Judith's voice grew steady as she continued. "I wasn't about to give him my hard-earned cash," she said. "He's young. He can work for his own money. I'm ashamed to say I lied. I don't like liars," she said emphatically. "But I didn't know what to do. I kept telling him I didn't have any money to give him, but he wouldn't stop asking, so I said a quick prayer and fell over, pretending to have a heart attack. I've never had one, so I'm not sure what happens, but I guess I got it right because he got scared and ran off.

"I got up, locked the slider, and called the police. An officer came right out. I'm going into the station today to look at some pictures. I got a good look at this young man, so if he's in their book, I'll find him. I feel sorry for him, though. He seemed nice enough. The way I see it, he just needs a mother's love."

Then Judith broke out laughing. "Can you believe it, Maxine? I was always afraid of having a heart attack in the middle of the night—and it turns out the one I staged myself saved my life!"

Reflection

You will not fear the terror of night,
nor the arrow that flies by day (Psalm 91:5).

Lord, I don't want to be afraid, but sometimes I am. Thank you for being with me and in me by the power of your Holy Spirit. Whatever comes my way, I am safe and secure in you.

Pistol-Packin' Mama

It was time to move. The day had come. Ivy was excited and afraid. She liked the idea of a new place, new people, new opportunities. But she was also apprehensive about the changes, especially at her age. It's not that easy to begin again at 70.

The moving men arrived early and were emptying out Ivy's bedroom faster than she could keep up with them. Odds and ends lay everywhere. She picked up one item after another and heaved them into whatever empty box or bag she could find.

"I spotted my Ruger Bearcat 22 target pistol," said Ivy, "and realized I better not leave that out in the open. I crammed it into a paper bag with some miscellaneous clothes and stuck it in my bedroom closet."

A few weeks later, Ivy was settled into her new home. She had unpacked the last of the boxes and crates and what a good feeling it was to have all this behind her. One Monday morning she decided to get acquainted with the stores in the area. She drove to the nearest strip mall to look for a hair salon, a dry cleaners, and a grocery store.

"I spotted the K-Mart at the end of the mall," said Ivy. *Great!* "I was thrilled to be able to exchange a blouse my friend had given me for my birthday. I needed a smaller size and hoped this particular K-Mart would have it.

"I walked up to the customer service counter and waited for assistance. While the clerk finished helping the customer in front of me, I dumped the contents of my bag onto the counter."

While waiting, Ivy caught sight of a twinkly-eyed baby and began making funny faces to catch his attention. When she turned back to the counter the clerk appeared frozen in place, her eyes glazed.

Then Ivy realized the clerk was staring at her Ruger Bearcat 22 target pistol! Ivy sputtered red-faced and tried to explain. "You see, I moved recently, and I put the gun in a bag in the back of the closet so I wouldn't frighten the movers, and it looks like the blouse I wanted to exchange was in the same kind of bag, but it's back home…in the bedroom closet…" *Yikkity-yak-yak,* she thought.

Her story seemed weak even to her. Who on earth would believe it, especially one involving a real gun! "I expected the clerk to call security at any moment," said Ivy. "I pictured myself rotting in a jail cell like a modern-day Annie of *Annie, Get Your Gun!*"

Instead, the woman's face relaxed and her blue eyes turned soft again. "It's okay, ma'am," she said. "If this was a *real* hold-up, I wouldn't give you a bit of trouble. I'd just ask if you needed help getting whatever you wanted out to your car!"

Reflection

But you, brothers, are not in darkness
so that this day should surprise you
like a thief (1 Thessalonians 5:4).

Some surprises, O Lord, are just plain fun. And some are absolutely frightening. Please help me keep my eyes and ears open to what you have for me so I will not be surprised by your call on my life. I want to be open and willing and quick to obey you.

Lovin' to Learn

Dancing Shoes

Dorothy walked the streets of her neighborhood every morning, worked out at the gym twice a week, and kept her weight under control with a diet of good quality meat and fish, fresh vegetables, and whole grains. For a 74-year-old woman, she was amazing to look at.

In fact, her sixty-something neighbor, Alice, had even noticed how in shape Dorothy was. Alice had not had the willpower Dorothy displayed, and she was, frankly, a bit jealous.

One day as Dorothy walked by her house, Alice stepped out the front door and asked if she could go along. "Great," said Dorothy. "I'd welcome some company. What's new with you? I noticed your grandchildren were over for the weekend."

Alice nodded yes, but she had something more interesting on her mind, something she wanted to speak about with Dorothy. She moved to the topic quickly.

"I've been wondering how you keep doing what you do—and more importantly—*why* you do it. I mean, excuse me for saying so, but a woman of your age—75, right?—it almost seems like punishment…"

"Not quite 75," Dorothy interrupted with a lilt in her voice. "Not till December 28. I'm in no rush to get there."

"You do very well—for anyone over 70. I see you stepping right along every day."

"Alice!" Dorothy exclaimed. "Is that a pat on the head I'm feeling?"

Alice's face turned bright red.

"I *have* to stay in good condition," Dorothy continued. "I'm in a tap dance recital next month. And in August Les and I are contestants in a ballroom dancing contest!"

"Wow!" Alice said with a smile. "You really do have a lot going on."

Reflection

Let them praise his name
with dancing and make music
to him with tambourine
and harp (Psalm 149:3).

————————————

I want to dance before you, Lord, regardless of my age. If my feet won't carry me, my spirit will. So take me in your arms, dear God, and lead me across the floor!

B.A. for M-O-M

Allison fingered the college applications her twin sons had filled out. They were ready to mail. Her eyes were suddenly misty as she glanced at the family photos lining the staircase of their family home. She remembered her boys when they were little tykes, still holding her hand and sitting on her lap. *Now they're ready to take charge of their own lives. Where have the years gone?* she wondered.

She poured a cup of coffee and sank into the sofa in the family room, awash in memories. She also had some regrets. *I wish I'd gone to college. Dad wanted me to, but I didn't see the point of it at the time. I was focused on getting a job, marrying Emmett, and starting a family.*

Allison picked up the catalog and perused the pages, checking out the courses and the requirements. Her boys had much to be proud of. They more than qualified for university studies. She knew they'd do well in college. They always had been serious about their work. *I wonder how it would have been for me? I was never an honor student—but I never failed anything either.*

The more Allison read, the more interested she became. Her heart fluttered as she imagined herself enrolling in college, walking the campus, attending lectures, serving on committees, planning a future she had never given any thought to before.

Why not? she asked herself. *Who says you have to be 18 to start college or that you have to be 22 when you're finished? Maybe it's the norm, but it's not the only way.*

Allison popped up from the sofa and grabbed the nearest telephone. Charged with adrenaline she punched in the numbers to the admissions office. Before she hung up, she had enrolled in college at age 50. She started with a typing class and a history course. Not too much the first time around.

Today Allison reflects on her first history test. "I was so fearful that I ran to the restroom every few minutes that morning." Just before entering the classroom she made one more stop at the ladies' room, hovering in the stall like a scared rabbit. "I was so nervous I couldn't unlock the door to come out. I didn't want to be late for class, so I crawled out under the door. I remember two girls looking at me like I'd lost it. But I didn't care! I made it to class on time and got an A on the test. Eventually I graduated from junior college with high honors and then received my bachelor's degree with honors at age 55. Getting old is definitely not for wimps. Neither is going to college!" she proclaimed as she pointed to her diploma on the wall in her den.

Reflection

I press on toward the goal
to win the prize for which
God has called me heavenward
in Christ Jesus (Philippians 3:14).

Lord, when I set my sights on you and your goal for my life, I am happy and content. What you call me to you equip me for. I never have to worry about not doing the right thing at the right time as long as I listen and follow your perfect plan for me.

Cookin' Good

Omana had never roasted a turkey in her home country of India, so preparing a traditional feast for her first Thanksgiving in the United States was quite an experience. She had married an American man and moved to his hometown, Baltimore, Maryland. The couple decided to invite his entire family and some friends for a real American dinner. There were 23 people in all.

Before buying the turkey, Omana prepared herself by reading the directions on how to cook it. "My American friend Bertha was visiting me," said Omana, "so we went into the living room to chat while the turkey was being cooked. All seemed to be going well until we began hearing odd sounds—like small explosions—from the kitchen. After three or four of these we ran into the kitchen to see what was going on."

Omana turned on the oven light and Bertha burst out laughing. "Then she stopped long enough to tell me I had put the turkey on its breast, instead of on its back. As the moisture turned to steam, it could not escape, so it exploded. I realized that a little knowledge—but not enough—can be dangerous!"

Omana pulled out the bird, turned it over, backside down, and continued the roasting process until it was golden brown.

"Everything went well from then on," she said. "And all the trimmings turned out too!"

What a relief. Her new family was proud of her, and everyone enjoyed a delicious Thanksgiving dinner thanks to their courageous new relative from India.

Reflection

Act with courage, and may the LORD
be with those who do well (2 Chronicles 19:11).

————————

Dear Lord, sometimes I forget that even something as simple as trying a new recipe or playing a new game or meeting a new person can take courage. And yet it does. I am grateful that you are here to equip me for each task and opportunity. I praise your name in all the earth.

Gettin' Forgetful

Everything in Its Place

"Nana, what are you looking for?" seven-year-old Matty asked his grandmother Esther as she searched under and around the cushions on the den sofa.

"I'm not sure," she said. "This seems to be happening a lot these days. I put down my glasses or my Bible or my special pen on a certain table or shelf, so I'll remember where I laid it. And then I forget which table in which room."

"I have an idea," said Matty. "Pick a room for each thing. Put your glasses in the bedroom by your bed so you'll see 'em when you wake up. And put your Bible on the kitchen table so you'll see it when you make breakfast."

"Good idea. Why didn't I think of that?" Esther ruffled the boy's curly hair. "Oh Matty, I wish it were that simple. For a seven-year-old it is 'cause your brain is young and alert."

"What's alert mean?" he asked.

"Means your brain is like a soldier standing at attention, waiting for orders."

Matty laughed and ran off to play.

Later that day Esther's daughter Carol stopped by to pick up Matty after work. Esther told her about the conversation she'd had with Matty. They both had a good laugh. Carol admitted that even at age 44 she was beginning to forget things.

"I walk into a room," she said, "then stand around wondering what I'm looking for. Sometimes I have to go back to where I started so I'll remember. Then I run to the room and grab the item before I forget again!"

The following week, Carol and Matty stopped by on Saturday. Carol was carrying a long cardboard box with her. She presented it to her mother. "Found this at a garage sale and thought it was a perfect decoration for your *bathroom* door," she said.

Puzzled, Esther opened the carton and pulled out a wooden plaque with large lettering. She read it aloud, and then exploded with laughter.

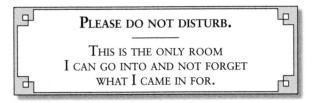

PLEASE DO NOT DISTURB.

THIS IS THE ONLY ROOM
I CAN GO INTO AND NOT FORGET
WHAT I CAME IN FOR.

Reflection

You will surely forget your trouble,
recalling it only as waters gone by (Job 11:16).

Lord, it's scary to forget things, especially when they are important. I remember leaving the stove on and forgetting to turn off the water in the bathroom, silly stuff that can be dangerous if I don't remember on time. But you know my weaknesses as I grow older. I'm reminded to lean on your understanding not on mine, and then I can relax and depend on you completely.

If the Name Fits...

Julianne is learning to cope with forgetfulness and having fun doing so. She lives in a Christian retirement community with more than 500 residents. Unless everyone wears a name tag (which they are expected to), it's a challenge to remember names. Some have a hard enough time remembering their own!

"I love the family feeling we share here," said Julianne. "People pass by on foot, on a bike, or in a golf cart or car and always wave to those they see. It's a good feeling to know so many men and women and to have so many know me. But names? That's my weak spot.

"Some people worry they're getting Alzheimer's disease, but since we are all name-challenged, we just laugh it off as another symptom of old age. Sometimes I connect a name with an old friend. Something about the person reminds me of his or her name. For example, one woman loves roses, and her name is Rose, as well. So if I can't remember her name I might remember the flowers she likes, or if the flowers come to mind first, then I can find her name right away. It's become a game!"

Others have picked up this game and use it to help their own memories. They've begun to make up names that fit various people's size or appearance or stature, and it's a lot of fun for everyone.

"Mr. Small is perfect for a short man," said Julianne, "Mrs. High for a tall woman, Mr. Watts for the gentleman who is as bright as a light bulb, and Ms. Young for a woman who looks ten years younger than her true age."

As Julianne read on a napkin in the dining room, "The nice part of growing older is that one meets 'new' friends each day."

Reflection

My purpose is to give life in all its fullness
(John 10:10 NLT).

Dear Lord, there are so many things to consider as we age. Something as simple as remembering the name of a good friend or neighbor becomes a challenge. But then I think, What's wrong with making up a new one? They both fit. I'm reminded of the fact that you are known by many names, including Abba Father, God Almighty, Comforter, Great Physician, and Holy One. And you respond to me regardless of the name I use. Thank you for making it so easy to get your attention!

Shotgun Wedding

Seventy-five-year-old Thelma was invited to her friend's daughter's wedding. Thelma's daughter, Marilyn, offered to drive her so she wouldn't be stressed out over traffic and parking. Marilyn knew from experience that her mother was often confused about details, so she wanted to be sure Thelma arrived at the correct location on time.

Marilyn made a point on most occasions of asking her mother for specifics so there would be no misunderstanding. However, on this particular day, Marilyn was in a rush herself and did not take time to look at the invitation or to question her mother. She simply got into the car and relied on what Thelma had told her during a phone conversation.

As Marilyn pulled up to the corner of Main and Fifth Street in the neighboring town, she asked her mother which church was holding the wedding. There were two on the same block.

"Right there," Thelma said confidently. "The white church by the stoplight."

"You're sure?" Marilyn asked when she didn't see any familiar faces in front of the church.

"Of course, I'm sure," her mother smarted off. "We're not

going to go through this again, are we? You never trust me anymore. I ought to know where my friend's daughter is getting married!"

Marilyn shrugged and pulled into the crowded parking lot. She circled three times before she found a spot. By then the two o'clock wedding was about to begin. Marilyn and Thelma hurried into the church foyer, signed the guest book, placed their gift on the table, and took their seats hastily.

As the music began, Thelma leaned over to her daughter. "I don't recognize a soul, do you?"

"No, but I figured Corinne is your friend so I wouldn't necessarily recognize the people she invited."

Marilyn slid out of the pew and walked back to one of the ushers. "Who are the bride and groom?" she asked. "I think I'm at the wrong wedding."

"Mario and Eunice," the man whispered.

"My mother said the wedding for her friend's daughter was at the white church at Fifth and Main. Now *I'm* confused," said Marilyn. "And we don't have the invitation with us."

"You might try the Lutheran church at Fifth and Manley," he said. "I'm a member there. It has a white exterior too."

Marilyn expressed her thanks, then hurried to the pew where Thelma was sitting, tugged her mother's arm, and motioned to the front door. Thelma followed, confused and upset.

"What are you doing?" she demanded when they stepped outside.

"We're at the wrong church, Mom. The bride's and groom's names are Mario and Eunice. Isn't Corinne's daughter's name Loretta?"

Thelma scurried to the parking lot, head down, muttering to herself. Marilyn shot out of the parking lot like a bullet from a gun, and headed across town to the *other* white church at the corner of Fifth and Manley, which the usher had directed her to.

When they pulled up, Thelma looked at her daughter with a sheepish grin. "I knew one of the streets started with an 'M,'" she said.

"Manley, Mom, Manley, not Main. And it's a Lutheran church, not a Methodist."

As they rushed in the front door five minutes before the two thirty wedding began, they nearly bumped into a woman with panic all over her face. "Excuse me," the woman pleaded. "I just found out I'm at the wrong wedding. I'm supposed to be at the one on Fifth and Main, and I'm not sure..."

"Mario and Eunice's wedding?" asked Marilyn.

"Yes, how did you know?"

"We just came from there. It's at the other end of town."

Seconds before the bride came down the aisle, Marilyn and Thelma squeezed into a crowded back pew and sank into exhaustion.

I should have asked, Marilyn lectured herself. *I should have asked. And I hope Mario and Eunice enjoy the cake plate Mother intended for Loretta and Ted.*

Reflection

Everything is ready.
Come to the wedding banquet (Matthew 22:4).

Lord, sometimes I arrive late for the important events of life, like prayer time with you, church on Sunday, or a wedding or birthday celebration. Help me overcome my malaise and realize that my presence on time and in place is not only a gift to you and to others but to myself, as well.

Music to My Ears

Erica sailed through the mall, browsing at the many kiosks loaded with various specialty items from earrings to teddy bears, from ice cream to cell phones. She paused at the one advertising a free phone and a no-risk contract. If she wasn't completely satisfied with the company's service she could void the agreement but keep the phone.

"Sounds like a great deal," she said, as she stopped and spoke with the young salesman. "I may need a bit of help filling out the paperwork," she added. "I'm not used to this. In the old days we just called the phone company and a 'telephone man' as we referred to the installer, came to our house and hooked us up. Next thing I knew I was calling my friend across the country. But of course that was many years ago."

"Nothing to it, ma'am. I'll help you with the paperwork. In fact, I'll fill out everything for you and set up your cell phone just the way you want it. You're going to love the convenience it offers."

He pulled out a contract and a pen and began asking for pertinent information. Erica stood close to the counter and answered each request.

"Now you can call your children or a friend across the country no matter where you are. As soon as we're finished here, you'll take your phone with you, and you can begin using it immediately."

Erica felt a ripple of excitement traveling up her spine. *What fun! I'll be in sync with my teenage grandchildren.* She could hardly wait to phone her daughter Nancy in Portland. Nancy had been bugging her to get a cell phone and e-mail so they could be in touch any time of the day or night.

"What melody would you like for your phone ringer?" the young man asked.

"You mean there's a choice?"

He nodded yes. "You can have part of the 'Hallelujah Chorus,' the 'Moonlight Sonata,' hip hop music, or a bell chime."

Erica laughed. "Oh dear, this is becoming more complex than I thought. Well, all right. Why not be a bit different? I've heard the same phone ring for four decades. I'll try something new. I pick the 'Hallelujah Chorus,'" she said and giggled.

A few moments later, Erica had her new phone and case in hand and the contract folded in place in her purse. She stopped for a Chai tea at Starbucks, and then she sat down to make her first call.

Nancy was thrilled to hear her mother's voice, and Erica loved being able to boast about her new purchase that she'd made without help from any of her adult children.

The following day, as she waited in line at the post office, she heard a sudden burst of music. *How amazing,* she thought. *The "Hallelujah Chorus" in the post office. Now that's refreshing.* The same portion of the score repeated three more times and then it stopped. *How odd! Perhaps the CD is warped.*

She didn't think another thing about it until she walked down the produce aisle of Super Savings Market. There was the

"Hallelujah Chorus" again! Erica wondered what was going on.

Then suddenly she remembered! Her new phone. That was it. The "Hallelujah Chorus" was the ring tone she'd chosen. *I've missed two calls. Now to figure out how to find out who called.*

Erica pulled out her manual, studied the section on voice mail, and called in for her messages. Both were from Nancy, checking in to see how she was doing. Erica walked out of the store and phoned Nancy immediately. When she explained what happened, they both had a good laugh.

The following Saturday, while playing cards at the Senior Center, Erica heard the faint sound of the "Hallelujah Chorus" drifting across the table. The other players looked up with puzzled expressions on their faces. Erica reached into her purse and pulled out her cell phone, confident by then about how to use it.

"My new cell phone," she said to the others. "Isn't it neat? I can't get along without it."

Reflection

Call to me and I will answer you (Jeremiah 33:3).

———————

Lord, it is comforting to know that when I call you I don't need a phone—cell or land line, and I don't need to listen for a special tone when you call me. We communicate with one another in spirit. Our wires never get crossed. Thank you for staying in touch with me even when I sometimes lose touch with you.

Every Vote Counts

"Rick, did you know Vince and Nadine cancel out each other's vote every time? She's Republican and he's a die-hard Democrat. I'm so glad we don't have that problem."

"Me too," Rick agreed.

Roberta sat back on the sofa, sample ballot in her hand. She and her husband went down the list of candidates and made their selections. Then they read through the propositions from A to J, and the arguments for and against each one. After they marked their sample ballots, they set them down on the bench by the front door so they wouldn't forget them in the morning.

"Thanks, honey," Roberta said. "It's so simple when we work together. I feel confident about voting tomorrow. How about you?"

"Absolutely! Now to pray about the outcome. Let's take a few minutes before bed to ask God to bring about his perfect plan."

"Good idea," said Roberta. Before falling asleep she made a note of each candidate and proposition they had decided on. She tucked the slips of paper into her purse as a backup.

The following morning the couple arose early and reviewed

their decisions while they finished their coffee and pancakes. They agreed to go to the polls and then stop at the supermarket for a few groceries.

Off to the polls they went. When they arrived, Rick realized they had forgotten the ballots. He smacked his forehead in regret. "Darn, that's what happens when we change our plan." They had walked out the back door instead of the front where the ballots were sitting on the bench. At the last minute they decided to drive instead of walk, since they were going to the supermarket right after voting.

"No worries," Roberta said, grateful for the extra lists in her purse, one for each of them. "I have spares."

They checked in and moved to the ballot booths. Roberta fished in her purse and pulled out a piece of paper folded in a neat square. She handed it to Rick.

She took out her list and was marking the ballot, when suddenly she heard her husband muttering aloud from the booth next to her. "Canned salmon, a quart of milk, salad fixings… Oh for Pete's sake, Roberta, this is the grocery list!"

A ripple of laughter echoed across the room. Roberta felt her face flush. "Hang on," she called. She finished voting, handed over her ballot to the volunteer, and then gave the correct list to Rick.

As they walked out, Roberta consulted her grocery list and turned to her husband. "I vote for a quart of milk and a loaf of bread," she said playfully. "How does that strike you?""

"Sorry to cancel your vote," Rick said with a smile, "but I have strong feelings for a bottle of apple juice and a bag of chips."

The two reached for each other's hand, laughed out loud, then dashed down the walkway toward the car.

Reflection

Bear with each other and
forgive whatever grievances you may have
against one another (Colossians 3:13).

Lord, how often I mess up, even with the best of intentions. I'm going too fast, or trying too hard, or thinking about one thing and doing another. It just goes to show me how much I need to rely on you so I won't waste time, make silly mistakes, and inconvenience others. Thank you for your gracious mercy. It is new every morning.

No Fries Here

Callie clocked out of the store at noon. She had one hour to eat lunch, run to the bank, pick up her dry cleaning, return two phone calls, and drop off a package at the post office.

She pulled out of the parking lot and onto the busy thoroughfare. The street was jammed with cars and trucks.

How will I get all this done and have time to eat? she wondered. *Gotta try. No time for errands tomorrow or the next day.*

Callie made it into the post office ahead of a woman with a luggage carrier loaded with five extra-large boxes. She had prepaid her dry cleaning so that stop took just a minute or two. She returned the phone calls as she drove from one place to the other, though uncomfortable doing so. It was getting more difficult to do two things at once. She had turned 60 the month before and suddenly she was feeling her age. She couldn't process things as quickly as she had just a couple of years before.

Callie pulled over to the side of the road and took out her to-do list to make sure she hadn't forgotten anything. She crossed off each item she'd completed.

~~dry cleaning~~
~~post office~~
~~phone calls~~
lunch
bank deposit

Callie was suddenly starved. *I've got to eat or I'll faint.* She spotted a Best Burger Drive-Thru near the bank. *Perfect. I'll grab some food then deposit my check without having to make an extra stop.* She glanced at her watch. Twenty minutes left.

Callie prepared her deposit slip while waiting in the drive-thru lane.

"Your order, please." The voice over the intercom brought her to attention.

"Double burger without onion, fries, and a Coke. Thank you."

Callie pulled up to the window, received her bagged lunch, and handed over her payment.

"Sorry, ma'am," the clerk said with a smile. "We don't take deposit slips here, but there is a bank next door."

Callie felt her face grow warm. She took back the deposit, grabbed a bill, paid for her lunch, and drove from the burger drive-thru to the bank drive-thru. *Maybe it's time to retire and head for the rocking chair,* she thought, laughing at herself.

She pulled up to the teller at the window.

"May I help you?" the woman asked.

"Double burger without onion, fries, and a Coke....I mean..."

The teller laughed. "We don't have a lunch menu here," she joked, "but there's a Best Burger next door."

Callie joked back as she handed over her check and deposit slip. "I should have known. Best Burger wouldn't take my deposit slip either."

Reflection

For six days, work is to be done,
but the seventh day is a Sabbath of rest,
holy to the LORD (Exodus 31:15).

Lord, thank you that when I rush through life trying to make things happen, you are there to remind me of what is most important—taking time to rest in you.

Good Ol' Days

Rare Treat

G ail shared a funny story that showed the difference between today and yesterday, when she was a young girl.

Her mother walked into a local drugstore one day during the 1940s with Gail and her brother, both elementary school-aged children at the time.

The pharmacist stepped out from behind the counter. He looked both ways as if he had a top secret. Then he turned to Gail's mother and leaned in. "I received a small shipment. Would you like to be included? I can only let you have six though."

Gail's mother nodded, delighted to be in on this order. She reached into her purse and pulled out a dollar. She handed the bill to the pharmacist, and he tucked it into his pocket. Gail then followed the man behind the counter, returning with a small unmarked brown bag. The transaction was complete.

"In today's world," Gail said, "we would conclude it was an illegal drug buy. But when this incident occurred, World War II was still going on, and many common staples were restricted. That made this shipment all the more special. It contained a few boxes of Hershey candy bars. Chocolate was scarce then, and only regular customers were included in the delivery."

"We hoarded them," said Gail, "dividing each bar three ways, one at a time over several days, for a special treat.

"Luckily for the rest of us, Dad didn't like chocolate. We kids and Mom didn't mind," she added. "That meant more for us. Yum!"

Gail says to this day she loves Hershey's chocolate. It's a lovely memory of the innocent days of her childhood and of her mother who looked out for her so well.

Reflection

Her children arise and call her blessed
(Proverbs 31:28).

Lord, what fun it is as parents to bring treats to our children and grandchildren. But even more special are the treats you provide—grace, peace, mercy, provision, your love and protection. A candy bar is delicious in the moment, but your treats last for eternity.

Musical Hit Parade

Monique was invited to present a program of piano music at a retirement home. She selected popular songs of the 1930s and 1940s, some favorite hymns, and patriotic numbers that residents could relate to.

"While playing hymns," said Monique, "I had a strange feeling someone was standing behind me. I glanced back to see a frail, silver-haired man glancing over my shoulder, much like my father used to do when I played and sang his favorite songs at home."

Monique nodded and smiled, encouraging the elderly gentleman to join in. He smiled back and started singing along in a soft, tremulous voice. He knew every word of the venerable hymn. "His eye is on the sparrow, and I know He watches me," we sang.

"The audience sat in rapt silence as he asked me to play more and more of his favorites. There was no question that he was having a wonderful time singing the hymns of his youth."

He was not the only one having a good time. Monique's eyes glistened as she played and recalled the happy memories of her childhood. "It was pure serendipity for me," she added. "I felt as if I were at home again, hearing Daddy singing his special songs while I played the piano for him."

Soon Monique, the man beside her, and the entire roomful of white and silver-haired men and women, some in wheelchairs, others seated at tables, some hobbling across the room with the help of a walker or cane, joined in until the retirement home rocked with the sounds of praise and thanksgiving to the God they loved and served.

Reflection

Moses replied: It is not the sound of victory,
it is not the sound of defeat;
it is the sound of singing
that I hear (Exodus 32:18).

Dear Lord, you love it when we praise you with singing and dancing and the sound of instruments glorifying your holy name. Whether we are young and robust, or elderly and frail, we can lift you up and honor your presence with songs of joy and gratitude.

A Little Compromising

Pie in the Sky

osemary walked into the den and stepped over the scattered piles of paper on the floor and two pairs of sneakers. She noticed last year's winter jacket still hanging on the back of the spare chair. She stuck her head between the computer screen and her husband's face. Max looked up, startled.

"What's going on?" he asked. "You can see I'm working."

"My point exactly," Rosemary replied. "*You're* working and I'm not. I need my own computer and my own desk in my own quiet space. Please, Max. The time for sharing is over. Surely you agree. I like my space nice and neat, and you like yours, well, let's just say you're more casual than I am. I could set up in the alcove off our bedroom. What do you say?"

"I'll think about it," said Max, feigning authority over the matter.

Rosemary sighed and walked out of the room. She knew it wouldn't do any good to press her point when he was "working."

That evening after dinner, Max opened a conversation. "Been thinking about what you said earlier. Maybe it *is* time to get you that computer and desk," he said. "I'll make you a deal—one you can't refuse," he added, raising and lowering his eyebrows a la Groucho Marx.

"And the deal is?" Rosemary probed, suspicious of her husband's tactics.

"It's peach season," he started, "and I'm hankering for some of your delicious homemade peach cobbler with real whipped cream."

"*Deal!*" shouted Rosemary, as she threw herself into her husband's lap and smothered him with kisses.

The next day, Rosemary and Max shopped for a new desk, a new computer, a pound of peaches, and real whipped cream!

Reflection
Be kind and compassionate
to one another (Ephesians 4:32).

Lord, when I want something I don't have to bargain with you or make a deal. I can simply ask and receive because you have come to give me life in all its fullness. It is your pleasure to give me the kingdom because I am the apple of your eye.

Night Out

ary approached his wife, Joann, as she settled into her recliner in the den. "Want to do something tonight?"

"Like what?"

"I don't know. Maybe a movie, or a drive around the lake, or even dancing at the Mayfair Lounge."

"Sorry to be a party-pooper," Joann said, "but I'd rather stay home. I don't feel like getting dressed and fighting traffic."

Gary shrugged, grabbed the remote, and turned on the History channel. "Maybe something here will hold our interest," he said and settled into his easy chair.

Joann offered to make a pitcher of lemonade and pop some corn.

"Not *another* program on World War II!" Gary exclaimed. He surfed the channels and then suddenly stood up and pulled Joann by the hand.

"This is pathetic! Let's *do* something. If you don't want to see a movie or go dancing, how about walking through Barnes & Noble? We can browse the travel books, get a cup of mocha in their cafe, and read a few magazines. Beats falling asleep in front of the tube like an old couple!"

Joann agreed as long as she could wear what she had on—jeans and a T-shirt.

"You look fine," said Gary. "It's just a bookstore, not a resort."

The two drove to the mall and walked into the store. They agreed to split up for a few minutes, each visiting a favorite aisle, and then meet in the travel section. Gary combed the gardening books while Joann looked at the self-help titles.

Twenty minutes later they picked out a couple of travel books to study, and Joann plopped down in one of the comfy chairs near the cafe. Gary ordered two mochas. When he returned to Joann, she was nodding off. He sat down next to her and realized he couldn't shake his own sleepiness.

"So much for a night on the town," he muttered, laughing to himself. He stood up, tapped his wife on the shoulder, and said, "Let's go. We can do *this* at home. "

They pulled into their garage a few minutes later, padded into the den, sank into their recliners, and broke out laughing. There they were—back where they had started from.

Gary flipped on the History channel willing to give it one more chance.

"I think I'll make some popcorn," Joann quipped, then put her head back. Within minutes Gary heard her snoring softly.

Reflection

Now may the Lord of peace himself
give you peace at all times and
in every way (2 Thessalonians 3:16).

Dear Lord, I thank you that I can rest in peace in my home with the spouse you gave me. How good it is to take it easy after a long day and to be content with what I have and with who I am.

This Old House

Helen, at age 65, wanted to buy a house of her own. The very idea gave her a nervous twitch and a delightful thrill. She appreciated that her daughter and son-in-law had shared their acreage with her for the past five years. They respected her privacy, and she had no financial worries or concerns about a leaky roof or frozen pipe. But Helen couldn't shake the longing to have a place of her very own, where she could entertain friends, spread out her mementos, plant roses and tulips, and invite out-of-town family to visit.

She toyed with the idea back and forth. One day she was content with what she had, and the next day the longing for her own home returned. She decided to take care of business right then. No more waffling. She'd call a Realtor and start looking.

That action step should help me make a firm decision one way or the other, she mused.

The first day out, the Realtor parked in front of a house with two tall oaks in front and on the side. Rhododendrons edged the foundation and a beautiful maple tree set off the backyard. The house was on a quiet street with a cul-de-sac that opened to miles of swaying grass on the wetlands. And it was just a short walk to the bay that stretched 22 miles across.

Helen stood there imagining her grandchildren and Elizabeth, her Pomeranian, playing in the fenced-in yard and walking with her along the beach. "I tingled just thinking about it," said Helen.

"But then I walked inside and my heart sank. It was a disaster of dark walls, stained and worn carpets, windows broken or missing, and a door hanging by a single hinge. Fortunately the kitchen and breakfast room were a step up, with attractive tile flooring and windows that let in plenty of sunshine."

After looking the place over, Helen and the Realtor parted. They agreed to meet later that day. No matter how many houses Helen drove by, she couldn't get the little one by the bay out of her mind. The next morning she woke up, called the Realtor, and made an offer.

Then came the explaining—to her daughter Kay, to her sister, to her friends, all of whom had a reason why this was the most ridiculous thing she could do at her age.

"Mom," Kay asked, "why do you want to leave us? Who'll help you cut the grass? And what if something breaks?"

Helen stopped, looked her daughter in the eye, and told her the truth about herself at this crucial time in her life. "I've loved living with you and Ron. You've given me so much and I'm grateful. Maybe some day I'll return, if you'll have me, but right now, I'd like to be independent while I'm still able."

Kay looked at her mother. "Okay, Mom. I see what you mean. You deserve to have your own place. You are always welcome here, and I want to help you in any way I can."

Two months later Helen was in her own house—the one near the bay that simply needed a little fixing up. She had planned to hire a painter and a gardener and a fix-it man, but none of that was necessary. The day after she signed the final documents, her four children, her sisters, her brothers, and all their families converged at the property and began shouting one over the other.

"We're painting the house."

"I'll replace the broken windows."

"I'm repairing the doors."

"I'll take care of the light fixtures."

"I'd like to mow the lawn."

And so it began. Two weeks of painting, hammering, cleaning, mowing, and most of all, laughing. And two weeks of pizza and picnics on the soft green lawn under the shade of the maple tree in Helen's very own yard.

What seemed, at first, like stepping off a cliff, was actually a step into her future.

"I now have a renewed sense of confidence, enthusiasm, and gratitude as I look at the tulips and daffodils blooming everywhere," Helen said. "I love the roses climbing the front fence and the wisteria coming to life in the side yard.

"As the house was transformed, so was I."

Reflection

Your faithfulness continues
through all generations (Psalm 119:90).

Dear Lord, no one can outgive you. Thank you for looking after my most intimate needs, my deepest desires, my heartfelt longings, and then responding with gifts beyond my dreams.

A Note from the Editors

This book was selected by the Books and Inspirational Media Division of Guideposts, the world's leading inspirational publisher. Founded in 1945 by Dr. Norman Vincent Peale and his wife Ruth Stafford Peale, Guideposts helps people from all walks of life achieve their maximum personal and spiritual potential. Guideposts is committed to communicating positive, faith-filled principles for people everywhere to use in successful daily living.

Our publications include award-winning magazines such as *Guideposts*, *Angels on Earth* and *Positive Thinking*, best-selling books, and outreach services that demonstrate what can happen when faith and positive thinking are applied in day-to-day life.

For more information, visit us online at www.guideposts.com, call (800) 431-2344 or write Guideposts, PO Box 5815, Harlan, Iowa 51593.